Integrated Management of Processes and Information

Integrated Management of Processes and Information

Kenneth A. Shaw, PhD

business**expert**
Press

First published in 2013 by
Business Expert Press, LLC
222 East 46th Street, New York, NY 10017
www.businessexpertpress.com

ISBN-13: 978-1-60649-444-8 (paperback)
ISBN-13: 978-1-60649-445-5 (e-book)

Business Expert Press Quantitative Approaches to Decision Making
collection

Collection ISSN: 2163-9515 (print)
Collection ISSN: 2163-9582 (electronic)

Cover and interior design by Exeter Premedia Services Private Ltd.,
Chennai, India

First edition: 2013

10 9 8 7 6 5 4 3 2 1

Printed in the United States of America.

Abstract

Each step in a company's manufacturing, service, and information processes uses, creates, supplies, and stores information. In many businesses, the information processes are managed separately from other business processes. However, they should be considered together with other operations in a process to develop more effective and less-expensive methods for acquiring and using that information.

Using a conversational tone, the author discusses a number of the procedural and managerial policy considerations for small and large businesses regarding information technology, process management, and business choices. The discussion focuses more on informing the reader about process-oriented concepts and management options available rather than providing specific recommendations regarding which process or information strategy to use.

Readers are introduced to a few of the more commonly used process modeling methods and how they can be modified to integrate information considerations. The various categories and forms of information are discussed along with some suggestions regarding what groups of information to collect and methods for handling that information.

The conditions necessary for success when incorporating information software management packages such as enterprise resource planning (ERP), customer relationship management (CRM), and Big Data analysis are reviewed.

References are provided for those readers wishing to follow-up on more specific details regarding each of the topics. A glossary of terms and a set of acronym and symbol definitions are included at the end of the book.

Keywords

information processes, service processes, manufacturing processes, process management, information technology, enterprise software solutions, stochastic data, deterministic data, service blueprint, block diagram, cross-functional diagram, information flow, information transfer, information standardization, information medium, cyber security, value-added step, dematerialization, food service information processes, DSS, ERP, MRP, CRM, SPC, PDM, SaaS, Big Data, data mining, SMB, decision support systems, business intelligence, Shannon theory of communication, cloud computing, BYOD, VoIP, barcode, OCR, RFID, inventory tracking.

Contents

List of Illustrations

Figures

Tables

Preface

The impetus for writing this book is the result of a number of conversations with friends and associates, an accumulation of professional experiences, and, most recently, my interactions with business students and faculty regarding operations and process management improvements.

The increased focus on supply chain principles and their business considerations in a global economy has often resulted in less time in many business school curriculums for more in-depth coverage of specific operations methods such as process analysis, service processes, yield management, forecasting, and the effective application of information (the subject of this book). There also is little time for class discussions regarding the factors affecting the variability of the predicted results of such methods. As a result, these topics are often omitted or only provided as chapter supplements in recent editions of operations management textbooks.

To help address this situation in the College of Business at Oregon State University, I suggested to several of my colleagues that we should add a process management course to precede or accompany the existing operations management course. Prof. René Reitsma, who taught an introductory IT course for sophomores, approached me with the idea of integrating that course with process management topics to form a new core course as a prerequisite to the current operations management course. After some discussion, we also agreed to use service processes for class examples and exercises as the operations course already covered manufacturing examples, René championed the proposal in cooperation with another colleague, V. T. Raja, and got approval for the new course to be required at the sophomore level for all OSU business students.

This book combines some of the core content we presented in the course with some considerations and applications of more interest to practicing small-to-medium-sized business (SMB) managers and professionals. An earlier Business Expert Press book, *Waiting Line Applications*,[1] presents an in-depth discussion of the queuing process content that was included in the course.

Acknowledgments

It is important that I acknowledge the valued questions, discussions, advice, and inputs provided by my former students and a number of my colleagues, friends, and the staff at Business Expert Press. These individuals include:

René Reitsma, V. T. Raja, Michael Curry, Zhaohui Wu, James Moran, Bryon Marshall, Randal Smith, and Mark Van Patten in the College of Business at Oregon State University.

John Sloan, a long-time friend and colleague at both Hewlett-Packard and the College of Business at Oregon State University and current fellow culinary student.

James and Mona Fitzsimmons, who coauthored the textbook[2] we used for the service process content in the integrated information and process management course described earlier. They were the ones who inspired me to begin writing business application books.

David Parker, Scott Isenberg, and Cindy Durand of Business Expert Press, who provided encouragement, great feedback, and patience during the completion of the text.

Don Stengel of California State University—Fresno who reviewed the manuscript and provided useful suggestions.

Last, but far from least, I must express my thanks and appreciation to my wife, Judy, and our children, Rachel and Jeremy, for their patience and encouragement when I often worked long hours and some weekends to understand business processes better.

Introduction

Information is the lifeblood of business. Just like an adequate volume, composition, and flow of blood is necessary for life, a sufficient amount, type, and transfer of information is necessary for business success. To continue this analogy, it can be said that operations processes are the muscles of business because they perform the necessary work. Unlike in the human body, where both blood and muscle are necessarily managed together, many businesses now manage their information and operations processes separately. This was not always so, and this book contends that there are a number of good reasons for those businesses to return to more effective strategies that manage them together. This is particularly important when the product or service provided by a business is information itself.

At this point, it is important to take a moment to clarify what the terms process and information represent in the context of this book. A process is a sequence of actions required to accomplish some end result. For example, the steps or operations required to fabricate a product or provide a service. Information is considered to be a collection of descriptors derived from observation, measurement, calculation, inference, or imagination that can be communicated to others. Hence, one can observe from these definitions that information can also be considered to be the result of some process and its analysis, handling, and communication to others can also be considered to be the result of other processes.

While this book should be useful for individual contributors and managers working in larger organizations, the primary audiences are business students and professionals working in small-to-medium-size businesses (SMBs) where the level of pragmatism required in making management and process design decisions is necessarily higher because of more limited resources and available options. The tone is generally conversational and the content is more about things to consider when managing or improving information and other business processes rather than promoting specific solutions. A few examples are provided, where useful, to help in understanding the content and to provide some inspiration about where one might begin.

The discussion assumes that you are either a business student new to this topic or a working professional who has taken the initiative to increase your understanding of the process and associated information aspects of your business with the goal of either improving service, reducing operating cost, providing a better product, reducing cycle time, increasing productivity, managing risk better, or some combination of these goals.

If you are a business student, most of the content will be new with some parts partially familiar, depending on the prerequisite courses you have had. The discussion assumes some knowledge of basic statistics, probability concepts, and a working knowledge of more common Excel functions. Students should find the information in the appendices to be helpful.

If you are a professional in either an individual contributor or a management role, you have probably reviewed your old college texts, talked to some more experienced colleagues, subscribed to one or more business publications, reviewed the literature available in the local library, and used Internet search engines to find sites that might help.

One result for both students and professionals is that you probably noticed there is a wide range of material addressing individual aspects of information or process management, but the material on how to manage them together is more limited. Another outcome is that you often encounter a variety of unfamiliar terms, some that are widely used by the media and business IT functions and others that are internal shop jargon for specific situations.

One of the book's goals is to help you navigate through these apparent discrepancies, provide some useful definitions, introduce you to some new concepts that are likely to be unfamiliar, and, foremost, enable you to integrate the use of information more effectively with other business processes.

Chapter 1 starts with a review of how business processes and information have been affected by technological innovations in the past and how much of that change has accelerated in recent years because of ongoing rapid advances in technology and explosive growth of a global economy. An increased understanding of how some current management approaches came about allows us to make more informed choices about what to retain, discard, modify, or add to current strategies. Two examples illustrating some of the effects of these technological changes on processes and the integration of information and product/service processes are provided.

Chapter 2 describes the nature of information. Information types, forms, formats, media, transferal methods, and storage approaches are discussed. Some emphasis is given to the issues that arise when dealing with unstructured and other highly variable or unpredictable information.

Chapter 3 reviews some basic modeling methods for integrating and analyzing information and product/service processes. It should be emphasized that this discussion does not just attach a classic IT information flow diagram to a traditional process flow diagram. Some new nomenclature is introduced to help avoid some confusion that can occur when adding information needs and flows to traditional process modeling and analysis. The methods are not meant to be all-inclusive, but only to illustrate some of the basic concepts required. A subsequent book by the author to be published later in 2013 regarding process analysis and improvement methods that include integrated information processes will provide a more in-depth discussion of this important topic.

Chapter 4 covers how information can be acquired and handled by a business beyond the more obvious uses for accounting and daily operation. Some suggestions regarding some lists of data that could be collected for various data mining and decision analysis situations are provided. How a business can acquire useful information at minimum cost while ensuring timeliness and accuracy is discussed. The chapter ends with a discussion of some useful methods for handling operating information more efficiently and less expensively.

Major software implementations that can help manage the increasing amount of data required by today's businesses are discussed briefly in chapter 5. Software systems for Enterprise Resource Planning (ERP), Materials Resource Planning (MRP), Customer Relationship Management (CRM), and many others such as Big Data analysis and Decision

Support Systems (DSS) are now available in both large and small business versions. These applications can be of considerable benefit to a business, provided some important conditions are met. Otherwise, their implementation could cost a business a considerable amount of money and frustration without a corresponding benefit as evidenced by several horror stories reported in the business literature over the past few years. Some discussion of available on-line implementations and other services such as cloud computing and archival storage is included.

Chapter 6 focuses on managerial considerations regarding the integration of information and product/service processes in a business strategy. In addition to handling the daily issues involved with successfully using whatever application discussed in chapter 5 is used by your business, there are a number of factors related to maintaining information integrity and security. Some suggested policies regarding how to deal with data management and security issues and where to standardize on information formats and databases are reviewed.

When information is the product or service provided by the business, additional concerns must be addressed to provide a quality result for customers. Chapter 6 also discusses some of the better practices for reducing data variability, dealing with personal use of information at work, password management, e-mail retention, archival management, and preferred customer treatment.

A list of references and endnotes is provided at the end. Appendix A provides a glossary of terms; Appendix B lists the definitions for the wide range of acronyms developed for IT applications; and Appendix C presents some useful information, tables, and spreadsheet examples for Microsoft Excel$^{©}$ users.

CHAPTER 1

Changing Role of Processes and Information

The importance of information is underlined in many of today's businesses by the presence of an IT (information technology) or MIS (management information systems) function. This function can range in size from a single individual in a small business to a department as that business grows in size and then to a large internal organization, generally reporting to the top level of management, for enterprise businesses in multiple locations and having a large number of employees.

Now some of you may say at this point "Isn't the addition of IT functions what integrated information and process management means?" The answer is complicated because the role of IT functions is in a constant state of evolution driven by hardware technology advances, software development, economic pressures, security threats, and changing management strategy. These forces can drive an IT function to focus on directions that are not as in alignment with the basic goals of a business as they should be.

Evidence of less-than-satisfactory relationships between business operations and the IT functions abound in today's business news, literature, and satire. When a new CEO takes over a company needing some changes to improve its bottom line, the financial media often reports that one of his/her first actions is to reduce the IT staff distributed in departments throughout the company and to consolidate the remaining staff in the central IT function. What usually is not said is that the distributed IT staff had likely come about because the company's central IT function was not meeting the needs of the company's internal information customers.

To be fair to the IT staff, such a situation is not entirely their fault. Many basic business processes have not been updated to take the best advantage of the features current information technology can provide.

In addition, many workers do not have the level of knowledge to take full advantage of the tools available to them or to communicate effectively to the IT staff why the solutions provided by IT are not helping them to do the job their boss wants them to do.[1] These mismatches cause considerable frustration when small-to-medium businesses (SMBs) try to implement scaled-down versions of enterprise IT applications such as manufacturing resource planning (MRP), enterprise resource planning (ERP), customer relationship management (CRM), and vendor relationship management (VRM).

In addition, there is often not a consistent or established management policy for handling information across all functions of the company. Individual department managers usually have some rules in place, but the rules may not be the same in other departments they need to share information with. Having a policy that clearly defines what rules need to be followed by all functions is necessary for good information and process management, but insufficient if it does not allow for some localized policies for addressing situations not covered by the general policy. This is particularly true when the standard database does not have room for the extra information required by a single department. Many conflicts with a central IT function occur as a result of this situation. What SMB professionals should learn from these failures is discussed further in chapters 5 and 6.

Let's take a moment to re-emphasize that the discussion in this book is directed more toward SMB professionals than toward those employed by larger enterprise organizations. The economy of scale in major corporations allows them to develop strategies and functions that are not economically practical for much smaller organizations with limited resources. For example, having separate functions or departments to handle IT-related activities and strategies is not the norm in smaller businesses. SMB IT support often is on an as-needed basis from external sources or is assigned internally to just one or more individuals who also are likely to have other responsibilities to perform in the business. That said, the basic considerations for integrating information with other business processes still apply; they just require some modification when the size of the organization is considerably different.

A Little History

Given that businesses of some form or another have existed for more than a few millennia, the presence of an IT function as we know it is relatively recent—only a few decades. While computers, cell phones, and other common electronic information handling and computation devices appear to younger business professionals to be commonplace, that condition was not true for many senior-level managers and professionals who began their working careers before the 1990s. For those of us who gained our formal training in trade schools, colleges, and universities in the 1960s to 1980s, the pace of technological change has been staggering and the ability to process larger and larger amounts of data much faster continues to grow exponentially in both dimensions of quantity and speed. Keeping up with these trends and adapting quickly to them is an ongoing major challenge to businesses, government, and the public and a necessary continuous education requirement for professionals wishing to ensure the continuation of their careers.

A brief review of the history and nature of the factors and technological developments that have driven and affected the relationship changes between IT and other business processes will provide some background understanding and help set the context for our discussion later about future needs and strategies. While some advances initially were innovations searching for an application or driven by governmental and military needs, most of the later advances are results of the ongoing desire by businesses to perform necessary activities faster, cheaper, or more efficiently and accurately. These factors and developments, in rough chronological order, are as follows:

- Development of devices for the government to handle large amounts of data faster and perform more accurate and complex computation;
- Basic theory and analysis of an information communication system
- Use of mainframe computers by large commercial organizations;
- Development of programming languages;
- Establishment of internal functions to manage data processing assets and technical skills required;

- Use of a network of terminals for input and output to a mainframe computer;
- Development of magnetic storage technology;
- Development of integrated circuit technology and the microprocessor;
- Invention of the personal computer;
- Development of spreadsheet software, followed by word processing, e-mail, and graphics applications;
- Establishment of an information-sharing network for research and government institutions—the genesis of the Internet;
- Establishment of satellite and fiber optic transmission capabilities;
- Expansion of the World Wide Web into the Internet;
- Development and implementation of broadband Internet access;
- Development and expansion of cell phone communications;
- Development of digital photography and the software to manipulate and transmit digital images;
- Exploding growth of global business enterprises;
- Cloud computing, virtualization, big data; and
- A return to the terminal and mainframe model using the Internet.

Author's Note: The dates quoted in the following history narrative are approximate. If one reviews references available on the Internet and in public libraries, there is often some conflict as to the exact date some technological event occurred, one of the many examples of the need to be careful in using data collected by others. In some cases, I am able to comment from personal experience that has included engineering contributions to and management of different aspects of these technologies and the rapidly changing IT environment. This experience has included not only developing and fabricating parts of the hardware such as integrated circuits, memory devices, and sensors, but also writing software applications for both machine control and data analysis.[2]

As populations and the businesses supporting them grew, the amount of data to be processed by larger institutions and governments increased to the point that manual bookkeeping methods typified by Bob Cratchit's employment in Dickens' *A Christmas Carol* were no longer up to the task in a timely and an accurate manner. Simple tabulating machines were reported by Pascal and Leibnitz as early as the mid-1600s, but it was not until the late 1800s that a commercially available tabulation machine using key entry, the Comptometer, was developed by Felt.[3] While Jacquard used punched cards as early as the early 1800s for controlling looms, Hollerith is more recognized for his use of punched cards for recording the 1890 US census data and inventing the tabulator and sorting machines to tally the data represented by the patterns of holes on those cards.[4] His company was merged with others in 1911 to form a company that later became the foundation of IBM.

Electronic device developments in the early 1900s for communication purposes also led to the development of analog computers for performing higher-level math functions such as integration and differentiation. This capability used electrical circuit analogs formed of amplifiers, resistors, and capacitors whose output voltages or currents represented the desired mathematical outcome. During the WWII era, the first electronic digital computers were created and the exact dates for some developments are likely unknown because they were developed to support military needs during that time. More familiar models developed after WWII were the ENIAC1 vacuum tube computer in 1946 and the first commercial computer UNIVAC[5] available in 1951.

A core concept of information technology often not noted in the business community was described in a landmark paper on communication theory published in two parts in 1948[6] by Shannon, an electrical engineer and mathematician at Bell Labs, where he considered the problem of communicating information quickly and accurately from one place to another (see Figure 1.1a). The basic elements are converting the information into a form that can be sent, a means of sending that form, and then converting that form at the desired destination into information that can be understood by the receiver.

This basic process has been used in many different ways by businesses and military groups throughout history to communicate between places and persons. Some examples are couriers carrying handwritten messages and maps, semaphore signals, heliographs, the US Pony Express, carrier pigeons, the telegraph, telephone, and radio. What became new with the development of computing technology was the ability to process information at

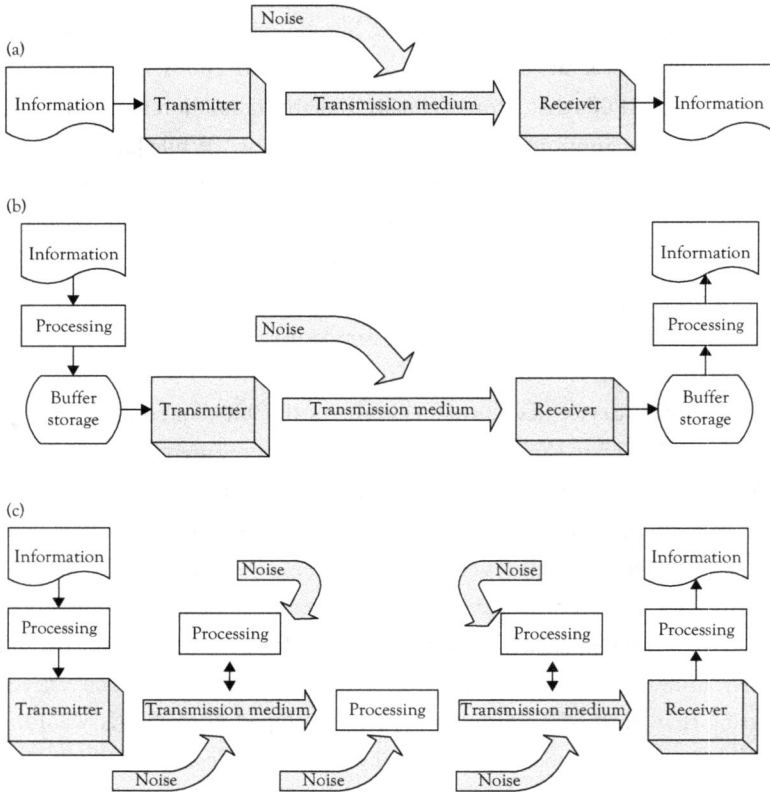

Figure 1.1. Evolution of information communication processes:
(a) basic model described by Shannon (1948), (b) model updated to
include information processing for sending and receiving with storage
buffers, and (c) a typical modern model including information
processing while in transit. While these models show only one-way
communication, they are also applicable to two-way communications.

the sending, transmitting, or receiving steps in ways that could speed up its transfer,[7] alter its content in a useful way, or increase its accuracy in the presence of possible disruptions (noise) during each step of the communication process.

The development of this ability to process information in new ways was supported by the use of mainframe computers in large institutions for accounting functions and research computations in the 1950s and 1960s. Because these computers required large capital investments, and new technical skills were required to operate them, departments were established in these enterprise companies to manage these assets more efficiently. In the beginning, university courses in programming and computer systems struggled to keep up with the pace of development in hardware and software applications.[8] Some progress was achieved during the late 1950s and 1960s with the development of software programming languages such as Fortran IV for engineering programs and COBOL for business applications.[9] By the early 1970s, more workers were able to access these mainframe computers using terminals with CRT displays and keyboard entry, moving away from the earlier need of preparing punched cards and paper tape to enter data.

The presence of what became known as IT functions in large corporations became more established as the number of computer users in a company multiplied. At this time the use of computers was still primarily confined to number crunching and managing sales and purchasing transactions. While some inputs and outputs were alphanumeric for mailing addresses and basic customer information, the use of spreadsheets, word processing, e-mail, and graphics was yet to come. The use of computers for managing communications would not have been possible without the development of faster and easier-to-use information storage technologies to buffer the differences[10] in operational speeds of computers, input/output (I/O) devices, and transmission methods as shown in Figure 1.1b.

This development initially was driven by mainframe users needing larger and faster data storage capacity for computation and record keeping. Writing data magnetically on ferric media replaced punching holes in cards or paper tape. Banks of tape drives[11] became common in many financial institutions and smaller, faster magnetic drum units were employed in research computers. Eventually, rapidly spinning magnetic disks replaced tape drives in the 1960s and, through continuous innovation,[12] became much smaller while providing significantly more storage capacity.

Transistors, used initially for low-power control and audio applications, began replacing vacuum tubes in computers as their performance at higher frequencies improved with advances in semiconductor fabrication technology. This reduced the size and considerable power consumption of mainframe computers and increased their speed and reliability.

More importantly, it allowed the use of thousands of computing elements within a single computer instead of hundreds. The development of integrated circuit technology in the 1960s allowed combining hundreds of transistors on a single silicon chip at first, then thousands, millions, and billions as the fabrication technology evolved to manufacture more devices per chip. This enabled the development of the microprocessor (a single programmable computer on one chip) that provided faster computation capability in a much smaller device and at a much lower cost. This also drove the development of semiconductor memory devices[13] to have a storage memory of comparable size whose write/read speeds could keep up with the microprocessor's computation speed. The same technology would be used later to fabricate the high-resolution image sensors used for digital photography. Without these design and concomitant manufacturing advances, it is hard to imagine how today's computers, digital cameras, cell phones, flash drives, and home entertainment devices could have come about.

How disruptive these technological advances could be to established businesses is demonstrated by the introduction of the first pocket scientific calculator, the HP-35, by Hewlett-Packard in 1972. Although its introductory price was about eight times the cost of a top-of-the-line slide rule, its computation speed, digital display, and range of math functions made it instantly desirable to engineers and scientists. Other manufacturers, most notably Texas Instruments, followed with similar versions, which helped bring prices down, and with the introduction in 1974 of a programmable version, the HP-65, slide rule manufacturers had all but disappeared by 1980.

Similar advances in graphics and printing capability affected the traditional drafting equipment businesses. The design engineering lofts of my youth containing rows of drafting tables, T-squares, triangles, drafting instruments, and India ink pens are all but gone in today's business workplaces, replaced by computer work stations running engineering design software and large-scale plotters for the decreasingly fewer drawings that are not sent directly by the workstations to CNC (computer numeric control) machines electronically.

For those readers whose working career started in the 1970s and 1980s, the heady days of implementing computer control systems and personal computers entering the business environment were challenging and rapid paced. Smaller computers such as Digital Equipment Corporations' PDP-11 and Hewlett-Packard's HP-1000 and HP-9825A became available in the industry in the late 1960s and 1970s for use as test system controllers or in factory control applications, replacing the previous manual or hardwired relay logic methods for controlling manufacturing equipment. This allowed more accurate and complex control that also could be easily changed to fit custom customer requirements. However, their individual cost and the user training required prevented their consideration by business at that time for general use in office applications.

When technically savvy individuals were exposed to what these smaller computers could do in their universities or workplaces, some of them began to work at home or in their garages developing computers they could afford to own personally and experiment with.

At first, the earlier personal computers such as the Apple II, TRS-80, and Commodore Pet were considered by businesses as only toys for individual computer enthusiasts. While a number of factors evolved that made these computers part of the business environment, the author's opinion is that the development of spreadsheet software such as VisiCalc was a major contributor. This software allowed individual business users to play what-if games with data in a familiar accounting format of rows and columns of numbers.[14] Once businesses began to invest in personal computers for spreadsheet analysis, the increased demand helped drive down the cost per unit and the potential software market size allowed other applications such as word processing and graphics to grow rapidly. Such applications allowed businesses to make more effective use of what was still a considerable capital investment per worker.[15] Significant contributors to these changes were the introduction of IBM's PC[16] favored by numbers-based businesses and the Apple Macintosh Computer[17] favored by graphics-based businesses.

As more and more information became available in electronic form, universities, research institutions, and government organizations began sharing data, developing computer network protocols and communication links to facilitate this need.[18] ARPANET developed by the US Department of Defense's Advanced Research Projects Agency was one of the first of these networks throughout most of the 1960s and is reported as first achieving multicomputer capability in 1969. A decade later,

USENET provided the ability for users to dial up using telephone lines to access information and post messages to others in user forums, sometimes called bulletin board systems (BBS), and newsgroups. Larger corporations with geographically distributed locations began developing their own private e-mail systems at the department level and these became more available to individual business users as personal computer installations expanded in the workplace.

The World Wide Web of information that had only been shared among large corporations, research institutions, and government organizations expanded to a much wider individual and commercial audience in the 1990s. Graphical interfaces (browsers) made it easier for users with limited programming skills to access information and view richer content. Processing speeds and the ability to handle larger amounts of data at the same time increased, allowing the use of computers to process data faster at the sending and receiving stages and now even during the transmission phase (see Figure 1.1c). These processing speeds often eliminate the need for buffering data at the transmitting and receiving ends. They also allow the monitoring and analyzing of streaming data in real time for a faster response to changing conditions such as bad weather along a transmission path or a significant change in the data reported by a remote sensor. However, this ability also increases the security risk because it provides new opportunities for unauthorized users to access and alter data.

A number of businesses began developing applications to serve this rapidly growing audience. While many of them who invested in the Internet financial boom during the 1990s did not do well, this activity helped establish the infrastructure of satellites,[19] fiber optic networks, cell phone towers and networks, and data compression techniques supporting the communication and e-commerce applications that many of us take for granted today.

The evolution of electronic imagery had its roots as early as the 1920s, driven by the desire to send images using radio waves or telephone/telegraph lines. Some of us had our first experience with electronic images watching Sunday afternoon Buck Rogers or Hopalong Cassidy serials on the small black-and-white screens of early television in the late 1940s and early 1950s. While some digital images were available on university and government databases in the 1970s, the common use of imaging technology in business did not expand until the 1980s when flatbed scanner development and printer output technology were able to keep pace with personal computer implementations. The real change that affected how we use and distribute visual information was the advent of the digital camera.

While integrated circuit technology was not yet capable in the early 1980s of providing a sensor with adequate resolution and exposure sensitivity for moving images, the situation changed when Kodak developed the first megapixel sensor using CCD technology in 1986. Little did Kodak realize that they had just set in motion the technological changes that would lead to the significant reduction of their core business in slightly less than two decades. Rapid advances in digital photography resulted in much higher resolutions and more compact inexpensive cameras in the late 1990s. A concomitant transition from analog video recording tape to digital media like CDs, DVDs, and flash memory modules made taking and storing high-quality images easier and more affordable. This transition was a major contribution to the changes in how we process, handle, and transmit information. In particular, it allowed the reduction or even the elimination of print media for communicating information. The impact of this on traditional postal, billing, advertising, and printing businesses has been significant and is still evolving.

Some form of global economy has existed even before the days of Marco Polo, driven by the need for some products such as minerals, spices, or crafted items that are not available at all geographical locations. Wars have been waged to obtain control over some of these locations. The rapid growth in information technology has enabled a corresponding growth in global economies, which has altered supply chain strategies in ways that are still evolving. Some major changes are the growth of cloud computing, use of enterprise-level software across many locations, virtualization of hardware systems, and the concept of Big Data. All of these trends have interestingly led some businesses to move their IT approach back to an updated version of the mainframe–terminal access model used in the 1950s. We will discuss aspects of this in subsequent chapters.

Business Process Evolution

How business processes are viewed also underwent significant changes during the same period; both from the influences of the same technology changes experienced by information handling, and by the change from a primary focus based on manufacturing a physical product to one more focused on providing a service consisting of mostly intangible items. As a result, process models must be updated from describing a sequence of operation steps to models that include organizational interactions, levels of customer involvement, peripheral support activities required, links to IT functions, and most important—the flow and content of information required by the process and its partners.

To illustrate some of the effects of these changes and the need to consider information processes more thoroughly with other processes, let's consider two examples. Example 1.1 discusses changes in a common medical procedure using some of the technological advances mentioned earlier. Example 1.2 discusses the changes in a common process model when the associated background and information processes are considered.

Example 1.1. Medical X-ray Process

Many of you have had an X-ray taken for medical reasons at some clinic, dentist, or hospital. If it was taken a few years ago, the basic process probably was something like that illustrated in Figure 1.2a. For a moment, disregard the physical activities required and recognize that this is basically an information process. The input is a set of instructions or request for information from the doctor and the desired output is the X-ray image of the area of interest that will be further analyzed by a radiologist. The transfer of this information is likely a written instruction from the doctor as to what area is to be X-rayed and possibly what the doctor wants to investigate or verify. The output is a piece of photographic film showing the desired image.

The process of taking the X-ray takes some time because the exposed film must be processed to develop the desired image and there is a reasonable likelihood that the X-ray might have to be taken again if the initial exposure is not detailed enough or focused accurately on the desired area, the developing process is not optimum, and so forth. Not shown are the background activities required for the successful completion of this process. These could include insurance authorization, maintaining an adequate inventory of photographic film and development chemicals, and some place for the patient to wait in case a retake is necessary.

Today, this process is likely to be considerably different and to take much less time in more developed parts of the world as shown in Figure 1.2b. The need for photographic film, associated chemicals, and a film developing facility is eliminated as a result of improvements in digital imaging sensor technology for X-ray exposures. This also

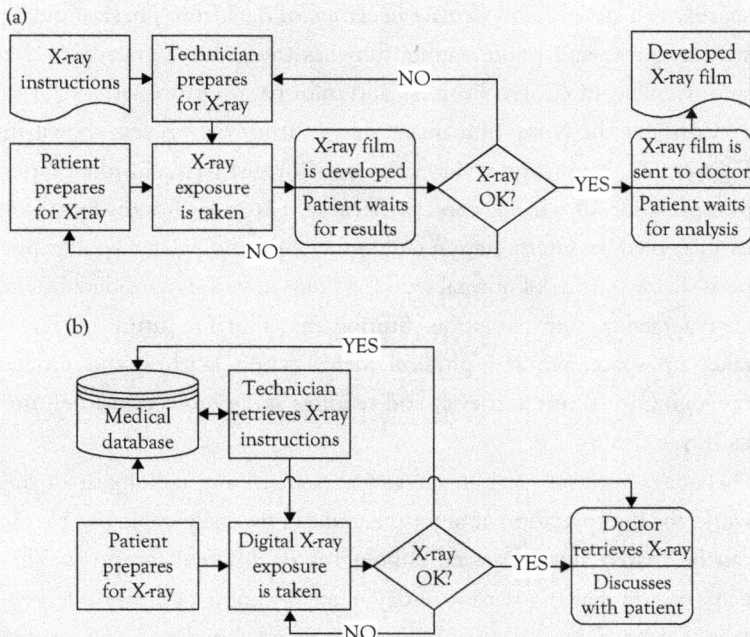

Figure 1.2. Evolution of medical X-ray process: (a) using chemical processing of the X-ray image and paperwork for other information communication and storage and (b) dematerialized information processes using digital imaging and electronic storage of data.

provides the advantage of an image that is electronic in nature. The percentage of retakes required is reduced with the only remaining major cause likely being that the initial exposure was not focused accurately on the region desired. Not so obvious is that the instructions from the doctor are also likely to be received electronically by the X-ray facility in an interoffice e-mail format. The other background activities are also affected. The insurance information is likely to be handled electronically and there is no longer a need for a separate patient waiting area for retakes because they can be taken almost immediately.

This example illustrates two important points. First, the way information is obtained is undergoing significant changes that allow a process to be performed more quickly, more accurately, and in a more usable form. Second, the more usable form of electronic data allows equally significant changes in how that information is transmitted, shared, and stored. This *dematerialization* of data from physical media such as paper and photographic film has the greatest impact on the improvement of current business and information processes.

Consider the X-ray film image output from the process shown in Figure 1.2a. It must be reviewed by a radiologist to obtain the proper interpretation of what it depicts. Because it is in a physical form not easily copied, its interpretation requires a local radiologist, who may not be available outside of normal working hours, a serious consideration in an emergency room situation. Storing that film for future reference takes up space, requires physical identification labeling and proper cataloging for future retrieval, and requires some protection to ensure its image quality.

Today, however, that image can be sent to any radiologist in the world for interpretation at any time and can be easily copied so that it can be shared among several radiologists in different locations. This helps ensure that at any time of day in any location a prompt interpretation of an X-ray is available for emergency situations. The storage space required is also reduced and has the added feature of being readily available to anyone in the world.[20]

Example 1.2. Fast-Food Restaurant Customer Process

As one of the work exercises in the combined process management plus IT introduction course required of business school sophomores at Oregon State University, I asked my class to get together in groups of two or three students to create a process diagram of the steps that they, as customers, would need to go through to obtain an order of food from a typical local drive-through fast-food restaurant. While readers from some parts of the world may not be familiar with such a business arrangement, the basic process for ordering food from a vendor, paying for it, and departing with one's order is fairly universal. A typical student group answer is shown in Figure 1.3a.

As shown, many students just connected the dots with a straight line. At this time, we discussed the importance of using arrows to indicate what happened next, particularly when a decision loop might result in an earlier step needing to be repeated, as illustrated in Figure 1.2a for the medical X-ray example. Like that example, the basic customer process at a restaurant requires a significant amount of information to be exchanged and processed. Most students usually recognize the need to tell the restaurant what they want and the need for the restaurant to tell them in return what their order costs. Students who are more astute include a step where they read the menu before choosing what to order. This is another information transfer step where the restaurant communicates to its customers what are the available food choices and their respective prices.

The student groups were then asked to consider what might be going on behind the scenes to enable the restaurant to process their order and to add those steps to their process diagram and draw a dashed line between their original answer and the added steps. This served to introduce them to a basic service blueprint diagram. A typical student group result is shown in Figure 1.3b.

Most of the students added obvious steps for cooking food, pouring beverages, and packaging their order. We then had discussions about whether each step was likely performed by a different person, which

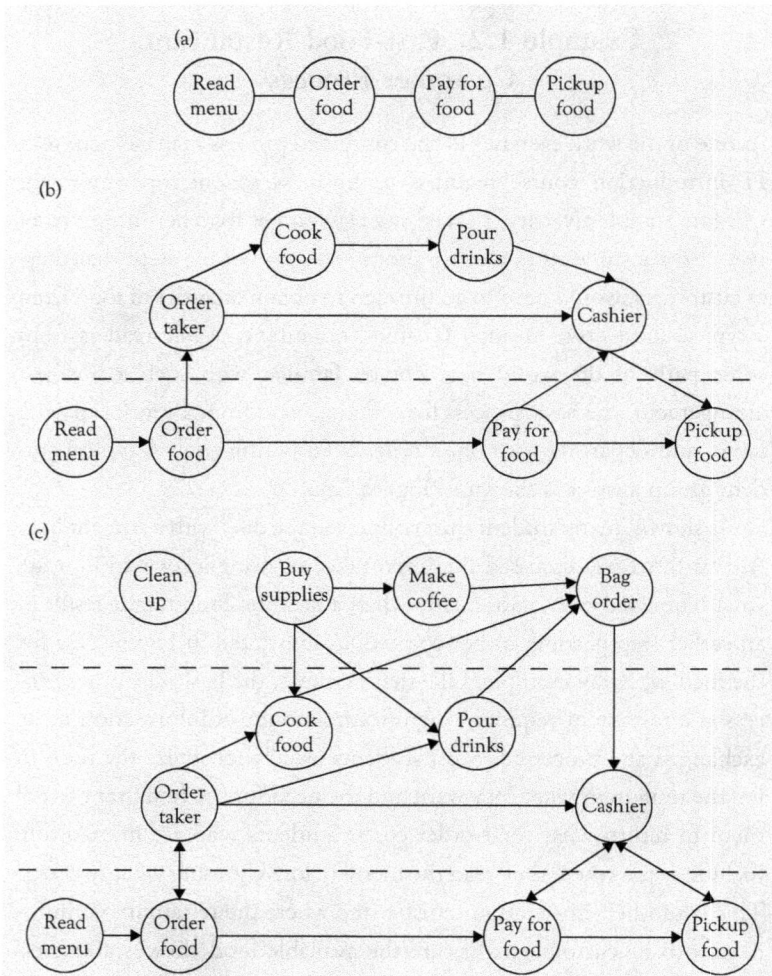

Figure 1.3. Fast-food restaurant customer process as modeled by typical business students: (a) initial model primarily based on what they as a customer would experience, (b) an updated model after they were asked to add what local unseen activities might be required, and (c) a more refined model after being asked to consider what might be necessary to support the steps in (a) and (b). Chapter 3 will discuss this process in more detail using three different modeling approaches.

steps could be performed by a single person, minimum staff required, and what information processes might be needed. This was followed by a discussion of the importance of somehow showing the information flow between steps or operations. Was the flow one-way or an exchange? Was a step a creator of information, or a user, or both? Was the information stored or retrieved, was it shared, was it duplicated? Finally, students were asked which step they considered was the most dependent on accurate information for the success of the customer process. Most selected the obvious ordering step, and some selected the payment step.

The work exercise was concluded by asking the students to give some thought as to what further background steps were necessary for the successful completion of the steps they had added to Figure 1.3b. Each group was asked to add those to their service blueprint and to separate those new additions with another dashed line for an expanded service blueprint. A typical result is shown in Figure 1.3c.

A number of students were likely to be stuck at this point because they had not yet become familiar enough with business processes to consider factors such as employee training, purchasing, work schedules, and so forth. However, they often recognized the need to have adequate supplies, utilities, and a janitorial staff. The information needs of these necessary background activities and functions are typically more complex and more likely candidates for the applications we will discuss later.

You are encouraged to work this exercise on your own, giving some thought to the information processes that are necessarily associated with physical processing steps such as preparing food and collecting payment. What do you consider is missing from these typical student results? What could be done to ensure the accuracy of the order information or the payment process? How would you depict the information processes on this service blueprint?

The two examples provided in this introduction illustrate the need to think differently about how information processes are treated in relationship to other business processes. To obtain the best improvement in both, their interaction and co-dependency must be considered as an integral part of any process analysis and improvement effort. A subsequent book will discuss the methodology for such efforts in more detail. Modifications to traditional process analysis and improvement approaches to integrate information will be part of that discussion. For the moment, let's return to our current topic of integrating the management of information and processes.

This can be difficult to do in some businesses with long-established IT functions whose purpose has not changed much from the days when their primary goal was managing large capital assets and technical resources to meet an organization's computation and reporting needs reliably, efficiently, and accurately at a minimum cost. A common strategy was to standardize databases and software applications, which worked well when the number of users in a company was limited. But when the number of potential applications of information processing expanded beyond payroll, purchasing, and sales applications, the one-size-fits-all approach began to frustrate newer users whose data needs, formats, and less structured information did not match the standards in place. Despite the grumbling among some groups that what IT provided did not fit well with what they were asked to do, the necessary use of terminals to access the mainframes in most companies helped enforce an approach of making do with what standards the IT group had established.

This grudging acceptance changed when personal computers capable of running standalone software applications were added to a company's information processing capability and began replacing the terminals. Now technically savvy users had the ability to get things done and store data locally, eliminating the need for mainframe access to do their work. This led to multiple databases containing some of the same information, but usually in different formats, making it difficult to correlate results among different departments and users. Different word processing and spreadsheet applications also led to electronic documents that could not be easily shared with others not having the same software. These disparities even extended to different printing formats depending on the printer manufacturer selected by a department.[21]

Some IT functions responded harshly to this chaos, persuading upper management to reinforce the standards the IT group had selected.[22] Others took a hands-off approach, focusing their efforts on their previous core responsibilities and leaving the personal computer users to support their own systems and to resolve major data conflicts between departments.

To alleviate some of this friction, many software developers and hardware manufacturers responded by providing translator routines or adapter modules to allow their particular software application to read documents created by other software applications and to print using a variety of printer protocols. The problem of multiple databases and different computer applications and hardware in different departments remains to this day. One can often read in the business news about some new CEO working to reduce IT operations cost by eliminating IT staff distributed in departments and consolidating databases. This situation illustrates a lack of an integrated management approach to information and other business processes. As discussed later in chapter 5, this lack is one of the major causes for failed or ineffective implementations of cross-functional software platforms such as ERP and CRM.

Some larger enterprise businesses have established MIS functions to provide more of a focus on the business information side of IT as opposed to a hardware infrastructure focus. In some cases, the MIS function replaced a company's previous IT group, particularly when the primary activity of the company is not manufacturing. In other organizations where manufacturing is a major component, an MIS function coexists with an IT function that handles daily operations and the hardware and network infrastructure. The effectiveness of an MIS function in either situation can be measured by how well it manages to avoid the proliferation of local lower-level situations described earlier, as well as its successful implementation and use of cross-functional software platforms.

Author's Note: The definition of what a function does in a company is often modified to best suit that company's needs. Hence, there is no universal definition of what the differences between an IT and an MIS function are. What distinguishes one from another is often blurred, accounting for the existence of only one or the other function in some companies and the presence of both functions in other companies.

CHAPTER 2

Nature of Information

What do we mean when we use the term information? Are we thinking about its content and form, or how is it processed or transferred? Defining information depends on the perspectives of the provider and the potential user. What is useful information to someone in the marketing department may be meaningless to someone working in the maintenance department. Yet, they both require some form or type of information to perform their respective jobs. In a recent paper, Denning and Bell pointed out that information processing technology does not depend on the meaning of the information for the technology to work.[1] The implication is that both information of great value and that of little value are handled in the same way by the technology.

The meaning of the information depends on the observer. I would add that it also depends on the provider of that information. Denning and Bell describe the situation we are considering here well with their observation, "Moreover, the concept of information seems fuzzy and abstract to many people, making it hard for them to understand how our information systems really work." Knowing what to measure and how to measure it in a useful way is a major challenge for many businesses. We will cover this important topic further in chapter 4 when we discuss how to acquire and manage the information needed by a business. For now, let's talk about what is information and how it can be classified and characterized, particularly for the best cost-effective use by today's enormously capable information technology.

In the context of this monograph, we need to recognize that for IT systems to process and transmit information it is necessary to convert that information to a format that computers and their peripheral equipment can use—that is, numerical values. This need for conversion is not only new and driven by the relatively recent development of electronic systems, but also a long-standing universal need to allow people to exchange information effectively. While we can compare two persons as to which one is taller when they are standing side by side, that determination is much more difficult when neither person is present, even more so if we may have not seen one or both of them in person. But, if we know their heights as measured in some standard unit such as inches, we can readily perform the comparison without their presence or ever having seen either of them.

In another example, if we want a color image that will appear to be the same no matter where it is printed or displayed in the world, we must be able to quantify colors in some way that can be used by different printers or displays to produce the same result. Moreover, that way should be easy to implement and preferably transparent to users.

Recognizing the need to convert between analog and digital information so that computers can process the information, move it from place to place, store it, and retrieve it for later use seems simple enough. But, and this is a big but, this sometimes is very difficult to do, particularly when dealing with complex data combinations such as images and books. Those combinations become much more difficult to define for search engines or to another person who has not seen the image or read the book.

So, what are the more important concepts we should be grasping at this point other than that data must be in numerical form for computers to handle it? First, if we can convert attributes and other descriptors into numerical forms, we can convert those forms back into attributes and other descriptors when we are done with processing, transferring, or storing them. Recognizing this allows us a wider range of choices and ways in how information can be used to improve business processes.

Classifications

To enable us to improve how we use information in our business processes, we need to increase our understanding of the nature of information. Let's consider the following list of possible classifications that we could use to describe information:

- Data type—number, numerical, digital, attribute, visual, code
- Format—list, tabular, chart, graph, image, sensory, aggregation

- Form/media—clay tablet, stone, etching, paper, tape, drawing, painting, photograph, digital, negative, voice, music, tones, odor, scent
- Transferal method/medium—hand to hand, mail, telegraph, radio, orally, telephone, television, Internet, e-mail, cinema, projector
- Purpose—instructions, records, measurements, acknowledgment, control, reference, regulatory, warning, information, menu, choices

To keep our discussion manageable, let's confine it to the major classifications, and you can add descriptors later to improve the match to your particular situation.

Data Types

We begin with a discussion of data types. Things can be quantified using numbers or numerical values or assigned attributes that distinguish one item or concept from another or at least categorize them into groups or sets.

While number and numerical values are often treated as meaning the same thing, there is a subtle difference in how they can be used. For example, a number can be assigned to an object (serial number) or person (government ID or phone number) to identify it or him/her as being different from another object or person. Numbers can also be used to indicate rank, class, or category according to some agreed-upon rules among the users of such information. Hence, the processing operations possible with such numbers are matching records in different places for the same object or person, comparison, sorting, and classifying. Numerical values come from a continuum of values that can be processed mathematically to provide new information such as averages, variability, totals, and so forth. Where these distinctions become fuzzy is when part of an ID number or phone number is used to also indicate the geographic location of the person when the number was assigned. While this was useful information in the beginning, it is fairly useless in today's mobile society. Another fuzzy distinction is when numbers are assigned to a survey scale where 10 represents excellent and 0 represents terrible or a medical pain assessment by a patient where 10 represents excruciating pain and 0 represents no pain is felt. In these instances, there is a temptation to calculate the average level of service experienced by patrons or pain level felt by patients. However, one has to question the usefulness of knowing these values since it is unclear as to how much the average represents the average of assigned values or the variability in the assessment process assigning those values. Furthermore, when dealing with individual customers or patients, one needs to recognize that each of them expects to be considered according to the level of their personal experience, not the average experience of others.

In chapter 1, we discussed the development of information theory[2] where the focus was on the elements required to transfer information from one place to another. During that same period, another often-referenced paper on the theory of measurement was published in 1946 by Stevens, where he defined four areas of measurement. These areas are summarized briefly in Table 2.1 along with some more areas such as log-interval, cyclic, and multidimensional added later by Stevens and others.[3] It should be noted here that the rapid advance of information technology will likely create the need for additional areas of measurement. Understanding the differences between each area is important because it affects how that data can be evaluated.

To emphasize this importance, I often asked my sophomore students to complete a simple assignment where they were provided several sets of data and were asked to analyze the data in whatever way the students felt appropriate and then submit a summary report in a manner that the students would expect their future bosses to want. Many of the students would jump right in and begin calculating averages, standard deviations, median, min-max values, and ranges without much regard to what the numbers in the data sets really represented. Only a few of them would think to graph the data, do frequency distributions, consider variances, or sort the data. Two of the data sets that they were asked to compare had identical averages, medians, standard deviations, and ranges, but distinctly different frequency distributions—one normal and the other bimodal. Typically, less than half of the students caught the difference.

As we discussed earlier, information must be expressed in a form that computers can compare (necessary for logic functions), add, subtract, multiply, divide, and, perhaps, most important, store. In a later work, Stevens

Table 2.1. Areas of Measurement

Area	Scale	Examples	Group values	Ranked	Distribution
Nominal	Arbitrary	ID numbers		Listed	
Ordinal	Assigned	Unweighted scores, pain level, address	Median Max-min	Larger or smaller, sorted	Percentiles
Interval (Dimension)	Linear	Temperature in °F or °C, time, distance, size, weight, duration	Mean, median		Range, standard deviation
Ratio (referenced to a defined origin or other standard value)	Linear	Rate, distribution, density, dispersion, temperature in K, age, frequency of occurrence (counts/reference)	Average, max-min		Range, variance
Log-normal	Calculated	Sound level			
Cyclic	Repetitive	Degrees in a circle, seasonality, frequency waveforms			Range, standard deviation
Multidimens-ional	Sets of above areas	GPS coordinates, xyz coordinates, polar coordinates, color component values	Hue, density	CMYK or RGB, polar or rectangular	

summed up on page 25 how to meet this need with his definition *"measurement is the assignment of numerals to events or objects according to rule."*[4] Other higher-level logical and mathematical computations are made possible using combinations of these basic operations in algorithms that perform logic operations or approximate various algebraic and trigonometric functions. Some of these functional algorithms are common power series expansions, resulting in defined sequences of additions, subtractions, multiplications, and divisions used to determine the value of a function using a single input variable.[5] The challenge, of course, is converting information such as the display of temperature in a glass thermometer into digital bits (ones and zeros) that computers can manipulate.

The rapid development of analog-to-digital converters and a wide array of sensor technologies since the implementation of computer-controlled manufacturing systems in the 1970s enable businesses and industries to meet such measurement challenges.

Attributes such as big, small, tall, short, red, green, good, bad, poor, grades, addresses, and so forth, are simpler forms of unstructured data because they can be interpreted variously by each observer or user of the data. Your perception of a tasty dessert is quite likely to be different from my perception of the same dessert, particularly if it is of a flavor that I happen to dislike. The color of an object as perceived by a human observer varies from individual to individual and agreeing on whether or not something appears to be a particular shade of blue is very difficult if there is no standard paint chip reference or ceramic tile of that color to compare the sample with. This becomes more difficult when communicating or storing information regarding color and more so when reproducing a color from that information. There are different formats depending on how the color is presented. Computer displays, on the one hand, often use an additive approach such as RGB (primary colors of red, blue, and green) where black is no presence of those colors and white is the full addition of all of the colors. Printers, on the other hand, have to cope with a white background rather than a black background when no color components are present. Hence, they use a subtractive approach such as CMYK (cyan, magenta, and yellow colors aligned with a black key). A black shade could be obtained by just printing all of the CMY components in the same place, but the black would not be as pure as just printing a pure black pattern (the key).[6] The ultimate challenge, of course, is being able to have a user's print output look the same as the display on the user's computer!

Like visual attributes, other attributes can be assigned numbers or alphanumeric characters so they can be processed, transferred, and stored electronically. Careful attention to these assignments is required because they are where many businesses encounter most of their database errors and inconsistencies. Although there are regulated standard units of measure for dimensions, weight, currency value, frequency, time, energy, and color, it is left to each individual business how they want to quantify or otherwise enter attributes into their database. To illustrate some of the difficulties, just consider how you would enter defect data for returned products or how to process customer complaints entered on your web site. Would a coworker enter the same information in the same way? If not, could you still analyze the information effectively? We will discuss this important issue more in chapters 4 and 6.

Finally, let's discuss coded data. While some may feel that coded information should be treated as a data format or form, I consider code to be a higher form of expressing information where additional translation is required to access the true meaning of the information. When information is encoded into bits and bytes of data (sequences of ones and zeros) the basic translation process follows a set of rules that are either widely known or can be readily discerned. Therefore, it is much easier for an unintended person to intercept, read, and even alter the information during transferal or access from storage.

Using Shannon's information communication process as illustrated in Figure 1.1, unpredictable disruptions or interferences in the transmission path are called noise. Some noises such as weather conditions or power interruptions over the transmission path can cause bit errors in the data, affecting its accuracy. Unauthorized access and alteration can also be considered to be a form of noise. It is also important to recognize the presence of noise in the conversion processes at both the sending and the receiving stages of Shannon's model. I consider the sending conversion to be the most critical since any error in translation here will be propagated through the remaining stages even if they perform their respective functions without error.

Two types of coding are used to combat these different types of noise. One is the practice of appending some bits of data called *parity bits* to each transmitted packet of data to help the receiver identify which packets were received correctly and which packets were not. This form of coding is used when reading barcodes to ensure the barcode is read correctly. A simple version of this is counting the number of ones that are in the data packet before it is sent and adding another one at the end of the packet if the sum is odd or a zero if the sum is even. The result is that each coded packet has an even number of ones and the original data can be recovered by discarding the last bit. The receiver then counts the number of ones in each packet and asks the receiver to resend any packet that has an odd number of ones. This simple scheme detects single bit errors very well, but is insensitive to an even number of bit errors in a packet. It also slows down the overall transmission rate when the noise level is high because of the many resend requests. More exotic error detection schemes such as cyclic redundancy checks (CRCs) have been developed that not only detect a wide variety of bit errors, but also provide the receiver with enough information to correct those bit errors without having to request a retransmission of the data. Modern computer disk drives rely heavily on this type of coding to ensure reading and writing accuracy. However, because these error-correcting codes are widely documented they are not effective at preventing intruders from reading or altering the data.

This brings us to the next level of coding designed to prevent unauthorized access to information. More commonly referred to as encryption, the rules for coding and decoding are either known only to the sender and receiver or are based on a process using elaborate calculations that can be readily solved if one knows the key. We will discuss encryption in more detail in the cyber security concerns portion of chapter 6. For the moment it is wise to recognize that given enough time any computer security setup or data encryption can be broken if an individual or organization wants to do it. The challenge, therefore, is to make the time required long enough so that it becomes impractical to make the attempt.

Format

As the amount of data acquired increased, better ways of presenting it were explored. Computer routines replaced the tedious manual computations required to translate columns and rows of numbers into displays of graphs and charts for faster interpretation and analysis. A useful reference for other ideas on how quantitative information can be interpreted and displayed is *The Visual Display of Quantitative Information*, a book by Edward Tufte. It was originally published in 1983 just as personal computers were beginning to make their presence felt in the workplace. Since then, Tufte has updated the original book[7] and written three other books on the subject.[8] All of them are useful reading, particularly the latest one in 2006 where he critiques and provides useful suggestions for improving many of the ways businesses present information. As an example, one of his ideas, *"sparklines,"* was first introduced by him in one of his forums on May 27, 2004. While small word-sized graphics have been used for more than several centuries in printed material and even in hieroglyphics to convey information, Tufte expanded their use to display extensive sets of data in a compact way for spreadsheet formats. He describes sparklines as *"datawords:* data-intense, design-simple, word-sized graphics." Their effectiveness in communicating information has resulted in their use in a number of publications and software data processing programs. For example, the 2010 version of Excel provides a function labeled "sparklines" in its Insert menu where the data in a range of cells can be graphed easily within a single adjacent cell to show trends in the data. Figure 2.1 shows two sparkline results on the right for the same range of data listed in the seven cells to the left to demonstrate how numerical information can be communicated as an image.

Another way to show trend data would be to use an Excel function to highlight each cell with a color signifying whether the trend from the previous period is up (green), flat (yellow), or down (red). This is referred to in Excel's references as conditional formatting or data visualization.

Other ways to indicate changes in data are different tones to indicate different operations or status, different vibrations to indicate the nature of an incoming text or voice message on a cell phone, flashing lights of different colors to indicate the presence of different situations, music choices to support different moods, or even odors to indicate danger like the additive used in natural gas to indicate a leak.

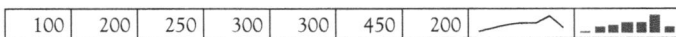

| 100 | 200 | 250 | 300 | 300 | 450 | 200 | | |

Figure 2.1. Sparkline example from Excel.

Aggregation is in my mind one of the most important formats for business. Although one of the Big Data rationales is to include more and more data for analysis, that increased level of details can obscure more obvious trends and imply a level of precision and accuracy inappropriate for estimating, forecasting, scheduling, or purchasing processes. Also, it requires more storage capacity, computing power, and increased data entry activity— all adding to operating costs to offset any perceived benefit. Aggregation is basically combining unit-sized data to larger, more manageable collections of that data. In its most basic form, it is rounding off data with decimal values to whole numbers when a fractional component is not likely in reality, that is, a fraction of a person, TV set, or keg of beer, for instance. A more practical application is combining data such as demand into quantities appropriate for handling, inventory, or purchasing. Examples are cases of wine, boxes of donuts, forklift pallet loads, barrels of oil, and tons or hundred weights of raw materials. Other less obvious aggregations are the total number of trucks, appliances, fast-food meals, and so forth, produced when the majority of their components and labor content are essentially the same. That is, tracking the number of black trucks sold does not affect how much steel or labor is required, only the amount of black coloring required for the paint. This is particularly true in today's supply chain environment where the majority of the manufacturing either uses all standardized parts or can assemble-to-order using a few special components from outside suppliers. In the latter case, those specialized items are usually standardized items for the suppliers and only need to be tracked by the buyers in whatever order sizes the supplier chooses to deal in.

All of these format possibilities can be used at either the sending or the receiving end of the information communication process described by Figure 1.1. To transfer information from one location to another requires some additional consideration of the form or media used for the transfer because some forms are not suitable for some formats.

Form/Media

The physical manifestation of information greatly affects how it can be used, transferred, stored, and retrieved. Long, long, ago in the Mesopotamian region of Asia, the Sumerians recorded information by making marks in a wet clay tablet, which when dry became not only a storage medium for that information, but also provided a means for transmitting that information from place to place. While considered to be a primitive method today, it should be recognized that a number of these clay tablets have survived for more than five thousand years and can still be read today by a few scholars, an achievement that today's storage technologies will find hard to beat when considering that the lifetime of their media is immensely shorter and the technology required to read it becomes rapidly obsolete in less than a century—78-rpm records, wire recorders, tintype photographs, 8-track cassette tapes, 5¼-inch floppy disks, Betamax video tapes, and 8mm movie films are some of the many examples.

Dematerialized information in its purest definition is a form of energy—light, heat, infrared radiation, radio waves, electric current, sound, scent, and so forth. In that form, it is easily transmitted, but very difficult, if not currently impossible to store for any length of time and not easily observed. Therefore, for most practical purposes, its definition must include the use of some physical systems that can process, display, and store digitized information electronically. For businesses using cloud computing resources that physicality is for the most part located somewhere else; so it could be said they have come closest to truly dematerializing their data.

Transferal Method/Medium

Information in material forms such as clay tablets, knotted string, paper, films, photographs, blueprints, paintings, tape recordings, CDs, DVDs, and flash drives requires physical transport by courier, horse, automobile, truck, train, carrier pigeon, plane, or rocket unless the information can be converted into some form of energy pattern that can be transmitted and received. *Hence, the form of the information determines how it is communicated and processed, not the essence of the information itself. Furthermore, the choice of which form to use for the information is the major factor affecting how fast and accurately the information can be transferred.*

The dematerialization of most of the information used by business and individuals has measuredly affected the methods used to transfer information in the past decade. Up until the mid-1990s, most of that information was printed on, transferred, and stored in the form of paper documents. In effect, we used the same transferal methods as we used to transfer physical products and the raw materials and supplies used to make them. Facilities were distributed geographically to shorten delivery time, both of products to customers, and to be closer to suppliers. A disadvantage of this strategy was that it was more difficult to share timely information among the various locations of a business. Overnight express mail services came into being for more urgent transferals of information paperwork such as contracts, orders, and invoices. The beginnings of text-only e-mail in the form of internal company systems for large enterprise companies that could afford them began to spread in the 1980s.[9] This enabled higher-level executives to exchange rough drafts of contracts and orders more quickly for review and initial approval before preparing final paper versions for mailing and signatures. Other, less urgent business information and information for potential customers (advertisements) were sent via the local postal service. For those of you who have begun your careers after the mid-1990s, it is likely hard to imagine how much time was required for decisions to be made when the time to communicate information was based on moving paper around.[10] Today's ability for businesses to use accounting services anywhere in the world and to have immediate access to operational data at any location would not be possible without the widespread dematerialization of information and the concomitant ability to transmit it electronically using microwave and satellite communication systems.

Some method of conversion has always been necessary to transfer information by some physical conductor or a nonmaterial means from one place to another. Before the recent electronic advances in information technology, this conversion was a tedious process and the dematerialized form used for transmission was difficult to store for later retrieval. Morse code in its simplest form used a person at the transmitting end of an electrical conductor or radio communication system to translate letters and numbers into sequences of dots and dashes using a telegraph key (often expressed as dits and dahs to better represent the difference in duration of these two basic elements of the code). Another person at the receiving end translated the resulting sound sequences created by a relay device activated by the electrical pulses into the letters or numbers they represented. The speed of transmission was based on skill, with a good person at each end being able to transfer information at a rate greater than 100 characters per minute.[11]

Today this process is accomplished at blinding speed using computers to translate the information into electrical signals representing the ones and zeros of much more complex digitized data. The technology that enables this to happen so that we can readily communicate all types of data with any part of the globe in a time limited only by the speed of light is far too complex to explain fully here. What does concern business professionals is its availability to their business. This is unlikely to be of concern to companies located in larger metropolitan areas, but can be a significant limitation to small businesses located in less densely populated areas where broadband and cell phone services are still sparsely provided. We will discuss these aspects in more detail in chapter 5 with other managerial considerations.

Purpose

The intended use of any information determines the best combination of type, format, form, and transferal method to use. Some information is more static in nature, has less time urgency, and may need to have some physical format for convenient use. Examples are a set of instructions, a user manual, safety warnings, restaurant menus, reference data, and archival records. An exception here is those records such as personal medical files and dangerous watch lists that need to be accessible quickly on a global basis.

Operational data used to control service and manufacturing processes must be timely, of sufficient accuracy and precision, and in a format and form appropriate for the application. Increasingly, this type of data must be online in digital formats both for automated manufacturing systems and for rapid service responses. Measurements of inputs, intermediate steps, and outputs of these processes are also necessary for direct control and for providing information to monitor process quality and improve process performance.

Customer information is becoming increasingly important to businesses. Initially its purpose was confined to payment, shipping, and warranty information that was easily handled in a structured manner. This changed when retailer, advertising, and marketing professionals realized they could combine increased IT computation capabilities with the dematerialized information stored in customer databases to mine such data for customer preferences, targeted advertising, and demand forecasts. This led to a number of new issues to address such as increased security risk, database duplications, errors, and storage capacity. These issues and others are covered in more detail later in chapters 3 through 6.

Information Characteristics

Each of the aforementioned information classifications can have various characteristics such as:

- Variability—deterministic, stochastic, probabilistic, random
- Accuracy—exact, approximate, estimate, tolerance, guess
- Precision—resolution, sharpness, fineness, level of detail
- Structure—structured, unstructured
- Longevity—ephemeral, permanent, storage lifetime, temporary
- Security—open, closed, secret, protected, encrypted

Take a moment and think about what you would add to these descriptors because the wide range of possibilities makes it easy to forget something. IBM authors use several V-terms (*volume, velocity,* and *variety*)[12] to describe data in their book on Big Data (Zikopoulos et al., 2012), a topic we will discuss in more detail in chapter 5. One of their sales representatives added *veracity* to these descriptors in a recent presentation about Big Data to IEEE members in my local section. I would add, with a smile? and keeping to the V-term theme, *value, variability, versatility,* and *viability* to the list.

Variability

At any given instant, a piece of information about an item or situation can be very accurate and precise, but an instant later can be another value equally accurate and precise if the item or situation is changing in some way. *We will ignore the variations introduced by measurement errors and other information acquisition methods for the moment, but will discuss those concerns later.* How much the information varies over time is described as deterministic if the variation is small enough to not affect the operation or decision using that information. If not, the information variability is considered to be stochastic, a collection of possibilities that usually have some boundary conditions but within those boundaries are unpredictable (occur at random). Occasionally we are lucky and able to observe that these possibilities occur according to some probability distribution. Such knowledge helps businesses make better decisions or develop more effective methods for handling such situations.[13] A common example is the management of businesses where the service or production process requires the use of waiting lines or WIP queues because the customer arrivals or processing times are stochastic.

Accuracy and Precision

When we say accurate, we mean how closely the value represents the true value. Precision is how finely we define that value. For example, 3.14159 is an accurate value for pi; 3.14159265358979323846 is a more precise accurate value of pi. A properly exposed one-megapixel image of a person's face can be an accurate representation of that person (barring the use of makeup, disguises, and so forth), but a 12-megapixel image of that person is a more exact precise representation. These distinctions are important because many people incorrectly use the terms precision and accuracy interchangeably. Thus, one can have a highly detailed image that is not an accurate representation of a person if it does not include a major portion of that person's face.

It is important at this point to correct any misimpression that accuracy and precision are independent concepts when we consider processing numerical information in computer applications, particularly when more complex mathematical operations than addition and subtraction are required. If two groups within a company start with the same accurate information, but use different precisions because one group prefers to round off numbers to two decimal places while the other prefers to use six decimal places for all of its data, the outcomes for the same decision analysis by both groups will differ to a degree commensurate with the complexity of the analysis.[14] As shown in Figure 2.2, this can occur in even a simple analysis such as calculating the area and circumference of a circle with a known radius. Here the value of pi is expressed according to each group's precision. The effect of expressing pi to 15 decimal places is also shown, because each group may use Excel's pi function in their

Radius	Pi	Area	Circumference	Precision
10.38	3.14	338	65	Two-decimal for all values
10.384379	3.141592	338	65	Six-decimal for all values
10.38	3.141592653589790	338	65	Two-decimal, Excel pi value
10.384379	3.141592653589790	338	65	Six-decimal, Excel pi value
100.38	3.14	31,639	630	Two-decimal for all values
100.384379	3.141592	31,657	630	Six-decimal for all values
100.38	3.141592653589790	31,655	630	Two-decimal, Excel pi value
100.384379	3.141592653589790	31,657	630	Six-decimal, Excel pi value
1000.38	3.14	3,142,386	6282	Two-decimal for all values
1000.384379	3.141592	3,144,007	6285	Six-decimal for all values
1000.38	3.141592653589790	3,143,980	6285	Two-decimal, Excel pi value
1000.384379	3.141592653589790	3,144,008	6285	Six-decimal, Excel pi value

Figure 2.2. Precision example using Excel.

calculations for convenience and are unlikely to recognize that in doing so they are mixing up the levels of precision used.

Some of you may be thinking that the differences in the results are pretty small, so what's the big deal? Among other effects, there are two important things to consider. One, you can observe that the differences are more obvious for the more complex calculation where the radius is squared to get the area. In computations where there are a large number of complex operations, such differences can be significant. Second, we need to recognize that we are dealing with computer systems and databases here where they are operating at their own levels of precision and when they compare results with the results from another organization they will report errors unless the software developers allow some level of difference to account for precision errors. As we discuss in chapter 6, this requires some managerial attention to setting standards for data entry across different functions in a company. This is not an easy task since businesses often must use information that is neither accurate nor precise, as they would like, usually because there is insufficient time before a decision must be made to obtain more accurate and precise information. In such cases, managers must work with estimates or approximations or just make the best guess based on prior experience. With luck, they may have some tolerances provided with these uncertain values to help narrow in on the best decision or operational setting.

Structure

Information is either *structured*, has a defined range of values or choices of values, or *unstructured*, where the range of values can be very difficult to define, those values can vary widely and unpredictably, and some of the values can be interpreted differently by different users.

Another definition for structured information is data that can be readily identifiable. The most common examples are information that can be used in spreadsheets, drop-down menu choices, and relational databases. Both numerical and attribute data types can be used, but the attributes must be either in a form suitable for sorting or comparing such as addresses and names or must be convertible to numerical values for a computer to process them into categories or distributions.

Most people describe information as either numbers (data) or words or both. Although they watch and listen to the news on television or the Internet, they usually do not think of images and audio as being the most predominant forms of information today for the majority of the global population. Analyzing, storing, and retrieving such unstructured information is much more difficult because of the wide variation in its content. Some progress has been made with image and audio files by assigning descriptive tags to provide some structure, but since the number of tags must necessarily be limited, most images are not described well. Again, some managerial consideration is required for a given business to be able to handle its image or audio data effectively.

Longevity

How long information must remain available or be retained is a major business concern and often a major operating expense. Some information is ephemeral, needed only for the moment such as asking a customer in a coffee shop if they want room for cream.[15] Other information may need to be stored for a considerable length of time to satisfy regulatory requirements or to provide a reference base for forecasting demand, long-term contract and insurance records, reviewing product failure causes, and so forth. These varying storage needs are an important part of information management, both to provide a business with the data it requires for successful operation and to support customer needs. More recently, longevity concerns have expanded to include electronic correspondence, particularly e-mail. In addition to compliance with changing governmental requirements regarding e-mail record retention, businesses also need to establish internal policies regarding electronic correspondence.

Security

Lastly and increasingly important, the security of information must be considered. Some information such as user manuals can be publicly shared without risk to the business, some information needs to be guarded to prevent a competitor from gaining useful knowledge regarding your business, and some information regarding critical assets such as customer ID data, financial accounts, and proprietary secrets must be secured. One negative effect of dematerializing information is an increased risk of unauthorized access and alteration of that information. Electronic forms of information are more easily transmitted, copied, and can be widely available. If connected to the Internet, such information is exposed to a worldwide level of attack.

Therefore, it is important for a business to classify what information can be publicly shared without risk to the business and to implement safeguards and access processes appropriate for the level of risk of unauthorized access or tampering of information that cannot be shared openly. We will discuss some of these strategies and policy considerations later in chapter 6.

CHAPTER 3

Modeling Integrated Information and Processes

If we want to understand the relationship between the services or products our business produces and the information that those services or products require for our business to be successful, then some modifications to the classical process modeling approaches are necessary. For the discussion in this monograph we will restrict our use to the classic block diagram commonly used for product manufacturing processes, a service blueprint used for modeling service processes, and a cross-functional diagram used to highlight different functional interactions required for a process.[1] Regardless of which process model you choose to use—one of the aforementioned models or another of the many models available—it is important to ask the following questions regarding each step of activity depicted in the model if you want to integrate information considerations into your process analysis. That is, what information is

- Required by the step?
- Created by the step?
- Processed (altered) by the step?
- Stored by the step?
- Transferred elsewhere by the step?

IT professionals and software programmers are familiar with asking these questions when they map out data flows to determine what hardware and what information processing capability are required. So, some of you are likely to ask one or more of the following questions at this point.

1. What about performance information for each step?
2. Why don't we use IT flowchart models for other processes?
3. Who is responsible for the information? IT? If not, who?

The answer to the first question is that performance information is often the major difference between IT processes and other business processes. Because of their different natures, what is an important performance criterion for one is not a concern for the other. To further complicate matters, different terms are used in IT and other processes to define the same type of performance. The growth of shop lingo in different functional areas and the extended use of acronyms in business, such as those defined in appendix B, are a barrier to integrating the management of information and processes.

Process performance is usually measured by the process owner in a way that reflects their major priority. A business whose competitive edge is lower-cost products will be more concerned about the costs of performing each step and the amount of inventory waiting to be processed. A business that competes by providing the fastest response will be more concerned about the time required by each step and process delays. It is not that other performance measures matter, but when resources for improvement are often limited it is best to focus on those measures whose improvement will have the greatest positive effect on a company's bottom line. Table 3.1 lists some of the common performance measures and some examples as to how they might be applied in information processing, manufacturing, and service functions.

To answer the second question, in some ways, we already partially use IT flowchart models for other processes because process modelers have adapted some of their symbols to more clearly communicate what a particular step in a manufacturing or service process does. Some common examples are summarized in Figure 3.1 using Microsoft® Visio®, one of several graphics software packages that provide business users the ability to construct various charts and diagrams. However, the information processing flowchart symbols lack the ability to represent customer interactions as clearly as they should for service process modeling, and there are a number of manufacturing process activities such as test cycles, robotic operations, and inventory processes that are also not well represented. In this monograph we will restrict ourselves to the use of the symbols shown in Figure 3.1. Some modifications to address the needs of a modeling approach for integrating the analysis of information process and

Table 3.1. Common performance measures

Performance measure	Information technology	Services	Manufacturing
Capacity	Storage volume Transaction volume User stations	Reservations, hotel rooms, airline flights	Maximum units/hour
Throughput	Bit rate Transactions/second Download speed	Customers/hour Customers/flight Customers/night	Units/hour
Response time	Access time Uptime	Waiting delay Shipping time	Lead time Shipping time Cycle time
Losses	Bit error rate Drive failures	Incorrect orders Satisfaction surveys	Yield Warranty returns
Cost	$/terabyte storage $/user station Broadband cost Software licenses	$/standard service Labor cost Variability cost for custom services	$/machine Material $/unit Inventory cost Shipping cost
Utilization (efficiency)	% buffer capacity % spare bandwidth	Overbooking Yield management Newspaper model	% Reserve capacity
Productivity	Transactions/server Orders /hour	Service rate	Units/machine Units/employee

other business processes will be suggested in a following book on the subject.

For more complete lists and standardized definitions of flowchart and process diagram symbols, see International Organization for Standardization (ISO), ISO 5807 *Information processing—Documentation symbols and conventions…* or American National Standard, ANSI X3.6-1970, *Flowchart Symbols and their Usage in Information Processing.* For a list and description of the symbols available in Excel, the online summary by Hebb is useful.[2]

The last question regarding who is responsible for information in a business has a number of answers, because typically this responsibility should be distributed, depending on a number of factors. *My basic guideline is to assign the responsibility to whoever has the most to lose if the information is incorrect, not available when it is needed, or lost. If the person lacks the technical skills to execute that responsibility on their own, then the person is*

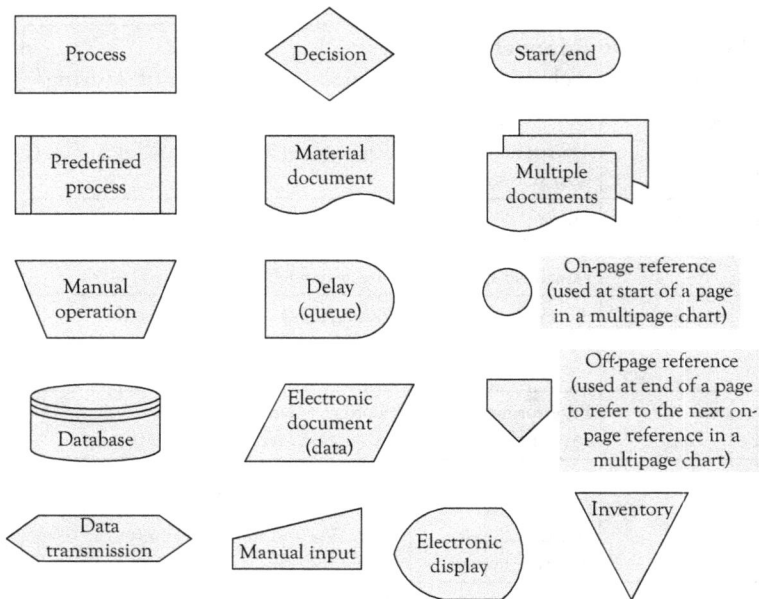

Figure 3.1. Information processing flowchart symbols adapted for use in other process diagrams.

expected to work with whatever IT function the business has or other sources, both internal and external, to resolve any problems that occur.

Whoever is in the best position to enter new information is responsible for its validity and accurate input. The reliable storage of that information for future use can be done by its creator if the creator is the only user, but normally this is largely an IT responsibility because most information is used by a number of functions in the company. IT is also responsible in this case for easy and prompt access to the stored information in their charge. Users have a responsibility for occasionally running separate checks to verify that the information they are receiving is true and still of value to them. It can be argued that IT should also be primarily responsible for providing technical support to the company's network structure and information security processes.

Assigning such responsibility and defining what that responsibility is to an employee is not an easy task. Not taking the time to do the latter part well is a major cause of dysfunctions between IT personnel and other employees. As an example, managers of departments where their employees are capable of writing software or macro functions generally have a difficult time getting those employees to document their code, either in comments in the code or in separate documents. When an employee is the only user of the code or macro they have written, it is often argued by the employee that such a requirement is superfluous and would take more time from other work the employee should be doing. If the manager agrees, then considerable difficulties can arise when that code or macro becomes useful to others or needs to be handed over to another person should that employee be promoted, reassigned, or leave the company.

Author's Note: Astute readers familiar with fast-food businesses are likely to note that I left out some activities, functions, or information processes in the following discussion. Some are intentional to simplify the discussion to more critical aspects of the process. Examples are omitting janitorial functions and other necessary maintenance and support activities such as human resources and payroll accounting whose daily routine is normally not affected significantly by processes involving customers. Otherwise, it would be very difficult to include a process diagram with such detail in a book of this size.

Because the fast-food restaurant business discussed in Example 1.2 has both service and manufacturing aspects with functional activities we will use it in all three of these modeling approaches to illustrate more clearly what the differences and similarities of these models are. Before we begin each model, let's review the basic elements of the process, including the information content. This is important to do first, because it helps keep our thoughts on track when preparing a process model. The elements for a typical fast-food restaurant are:

- Food preparation,
- Beverage preparation,
- Inventory management,
- Staff scheduling (we will omit this in our models for simplicity),
- The ordering process,
- The payment process,
- The order packaging process, and
- Quality management (often overlooked in process models).

The choice of a fast-food restaurant for these examples avoids some complications because the possibility of variations in the daily menu is considerably reduced. Seasonal promotions like eggnog shakes during the Christmas holidays are possible, but we will ignore them in our analysis, as their effect on the overall process would be minimal.[3] Because the menu is standardized, this simplifies inventory and purchasing processes. It also allows a make-for-stock approach where the cooks in many fast-food restaurants prepare frequently ordered items in batches during periods of higher demand like lunchtime. Beverages, however, are usually prepared at the time of order.[4]

When the customer arrival rate is low, food is usually made-to-order and a single person may take the order, communicate with the kitchen, collect payment, and hand out the completed order to the customer. When the rate of demand picks up, this activity may be assigned to two persons—one person taking orders and communicating them to the kitchen and the other collecting payments and handing out the food. During the busiest times, three people may be assigned to handle the customer traffic more quickly.

Observe the need for information about customer choices and demand levels during the day to determine how much to prepare in advance, and when. Is it best to analyze the process for obtaining and using such information separately or should it be integrated as part of the customer ordering process?

A similar question can be asked regarding the payment process. Many fast-food restaurants do not accept credit cards in the drive-through lane because of the processing delays during rush-hour periods, but do so inside. In our following models we will assume cash payments only, avoiding the need to show the process steps for verifying a valid credit card and completing the transaction or what to do if the card is rejected. Is it best to include such steps in the overall customer ordering process or to analyze them separately?

The brief answer to such questions is that treating such information-based processes separately is only effective if their choices and outcomes are independent of what else occurs in the customer ordering process. That said, my approach would be to first review the process in a standalone manner to best determine the independent elements like interacting with the credit card service and then consider the dependent steps interacting with the host process.

In the following three examples we will assume that it is the time of day when the customer demand is highest. Hence, we will have one person handling the order taking process, another person collecting customer payments, and a third person pouring beverages and handing out completed orders to the customer. A number of fast-food restaurants serving drive-through customers in addition to walk-in customers have three separate stations in the drive-through lane: one at a menu display for taking orders, a window for collecting payments, and another window for picking up the finished order. Inside the restaurant, there is usually a line for placing orders and collecting payments and a separate location for picking up finished orders. During busier times, there may be one or two additional lines for taking orders and collecting payments.

The food preparation area will be cooking food in a make-to-stock approach for frequently ordered items and a make-to-order approach for highly perishable or less popular items.

Finally, recognizing that many small- to medium-sized businesses still use paper as the primary medium for their process information, we will use that approach as the default method. An exception for the fast-food example is the use of a computer for inventory tracking and accounting data, now a common practice for businesses in developed countries.

Classic Process Block Diagram

Let's begin with the classic manufacturing process diagram where blocks represent activities or steps in the process and are connected in sequence according to the order that each step needs to be performed. When some steps can be performed independently in the sequence, we will use parallel or adjoining paths in the diagram. It is important to note that a block diagram does not explicitly show the overall duration of the process, although some users may include individual processing times with other information displayed inside each block. For the moment, we will restrict the block information to labeling the activity that the block represents. Figure 3.2 shows the process for a typical customer to obtain an order of food from the restaurant.

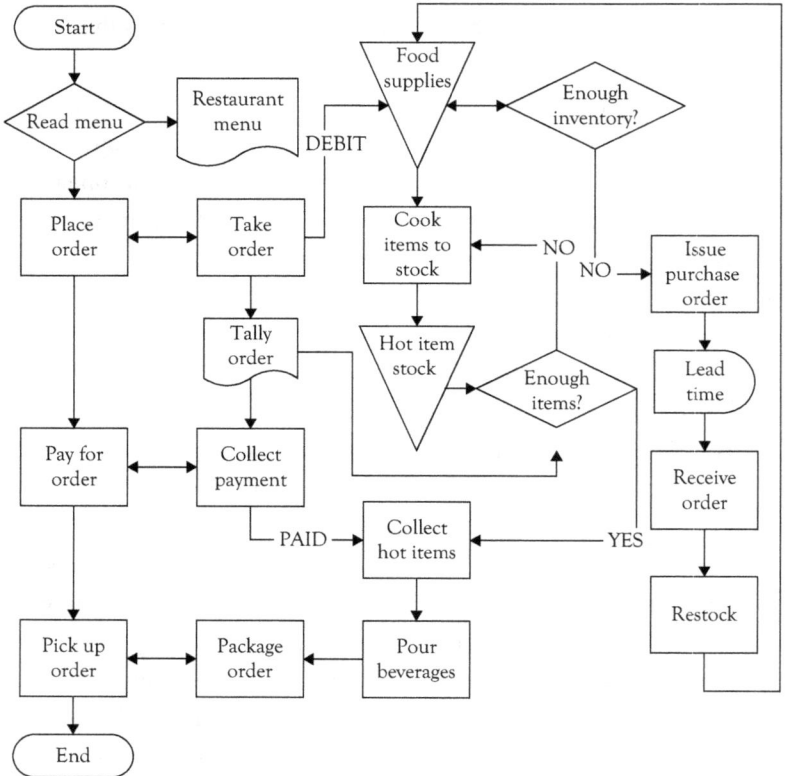

Figure 3.2. *Block diagram of fast-food restaurant customer order process.*

Service Process Blueprint

A service process blueprint separates the steps requiring some participation by the customer (called the front office) from those steps that are necessary to complete the process, but can be performed out of sight of the customer (called the back office). More advanced service process blueprints separate the front office activities into those steps requiring the participation of the customer from those that may require further participation of some of the customers. Some examples of the latter group are approval of additional repairs required, desired items being out of stock, credit card denial, and notifications that the order the customer has been waiting for has arrived or is ready.

As some back office activities evolve to use dematerialized forms of information, a few service process blueprints have separated back office

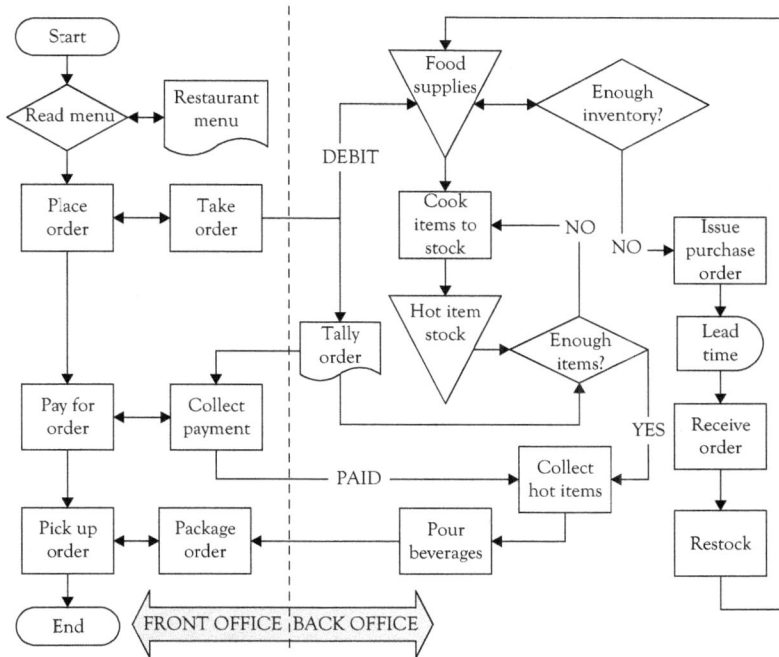

Figure 3.3. Service process blueprint for fast-food restaurant customer order process.

activities into those that need to be done on the premises and those that can be done at another location (usually information processing and many supply chain activities). These refinements to the basic service blueprint are useful when implementing enterprise software solutions for customer relationship management (CRM) and choosing what activities can be located elsewhere or subcontracted to other vendors, as discussed in chapter 5.

For our fast-food restaurant example, we will use a simple front-office, back-office service blueprint as shown in Figure 3.3.

Cross-Functional Process Diagram

A cross-functional process diagram separates the individual process steps into columns or rows according to which organizational function is responsible for executing them, with each column or row representing a single function. These are often called "swim-lane" diagrams because they are similar to the layout of a swimming pool for athletic events. And some of us call them Rummler–Brache diagrams because we were first introduced to them in a book on improving performance by Rummler and Brache.[5] While they called this method for depicting a process flow "a process map," by any name it is a useful tool for showing both the sequence of steps and which entity is responsible for performing each step. The cross-functional layout also allows the incorporation of when and how long it takes to complete a step by adding a time axis to the length of the rows or columns. In Figure 3.4, we show the primary support functions for a customer order—cooking, inventory, and purchasing. If we include the information flows, we would need to include an IT function.

Adding Information Flows to Process Diagrams

Some information flows are already depicted in the process diagrams when they are an important step and obviously essential for the completion of the process in our example like the customer placing his or her order with the restaurant, the food preparation area receiving the order, and the customer being told what they owe for the order. The service process blueprint allows easier identification of the more obvious information exchanges since they are an integral part of dealing with the customer's order and therefore are front-office activities.

The transfer of information to the kitchen depends on whether or not they have already prepared and put into stock what the customer wants or need to make-to-order what the customer wants and the customer should be told there will be an additional wait while they do so. Since the kitchen staff normally does not talk directly to customers, there must be a process for transferring such information to either the order taker or the person receiving the customer payments. Not so obvious is the need for inventory information to be updated as the kitchen uses up supplies and how and when that information is communicated to the purchasing function. If the fast-food restaurant is a franchise business, the purchasing group could be located anywhere. In such a case, do they get inventory needs through regular e-mails, database entries by the individual franchises, or by monitoring the local inventory directly using an Internet connection?

Although we have simplified the payment process by limiting it to cash payments, information from a local or centralized database regarding current prices is still needed to tell the customer what they owe the restaurant

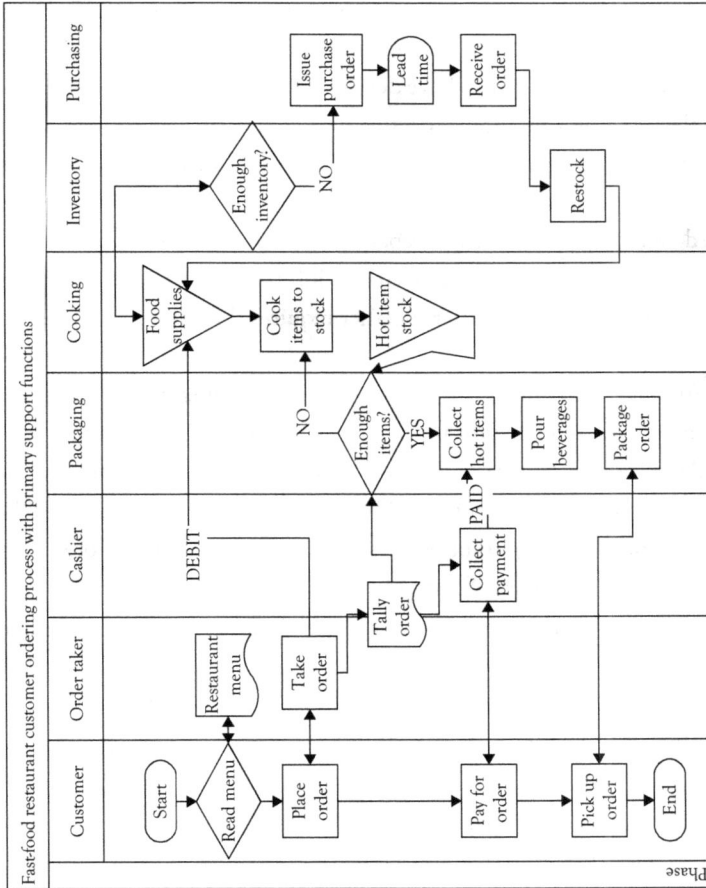

Figure 3.4. Cross-functional diagram of fast-food restaurant customer order process.

for their order. The same system is likely to be used to record point-of-sale (POS) data for accounting and tax applications, customer demand history, changes in product demand preferences, and so forth. Is that information archived locally or sent to some cloud application for processing and storage?

At this point, you hopefully should get the idea that there is a lot of information flowing around in even simplified process models and that most of the process steps for handling it are either not shown or are only depicted in very simple terms by users who are not familiar with IT systems. In contrast, IT functions are likely to have developed a very detailed model of each of the elemental information processes discussed earlier: inventory status, POS data, accounting information, and CRM data. Their models, however, are as likely to be as sketchy regarding the details of the material processes involved (verbally taking orders, preparing food, pouring drinks) as the typical process models are regarding electronic information processes. To bring these opposing viewpoints closer together requires three basic strategies:

1. An integrated management approach to analyzing, monitoring, and improving information processing with other business processes.
2. An effort on the part of business process owners to be more specific about the information needed by a step, what information could be provided by a step to other processes, and the usefulness of storing information as part of a step's activities.
3. An effort on the part of the IT professionals to better understand how the information systems they support can better meet the needs of the other process users with regard to availability, storage capacity, database design, and providing application support.

In many larger enterprise organizations, an MIS (management information systems) function has either replaced their former IT functions or exists in cooperation with an IT function to achieve these strategies. In SMB environments, these strategies are more difficult to execute because of limited availability of hardware systems and the technical expertise to support them and their applications to the business. Online resources such as cloud computing and networking support are becoming more available to meet SMB needs, but the management at such businesses should keep the aforementioned strategies in mind when selecting such resources.

Keeping the earlier discussion in mind, let's use one of the process models shown earlier to illustrate how one might modify a more traditional process modeling approach to show the information content of the process more clearly for analysis. Since all of the models have the same number of steps and the steps are all connected in the same sequences, we will use just the service process blueprint in Figure 3.3 for our example.

Figure 3.3 shows arrows pointing from each step to the next step in the sequence. In information flow models, an arrow represents a one-way transmission. In most real situations, the order taker repeats the order back to the customer to verify that they received the information correctly. This adds some time to the average completion time for an order and should be indicated by another arrow pointing back to the customer. In addition, if the customer and the order taker are not fluent in the same language or there is a noisy audio connection, this back-and-forth verification process could occur several times before there is an agreement on the correct information at both ends of the communication.

This situation also exists at other information transferal points in the process such as the payment step where the cashier tells the customer the price, the customer often verifies the amount, money is exchanged, change is counted by the customer, and so forth. Therefore, we modify the diagram to show these two-way communications by using two parallel arrows pointing in opposite directions. We could take this a step further to use arrows that also represent the medium used for transferring the information. In IT process diagrams, an arrow with a zigzag like a lightning bolt in the middle of the arrow, as shown in Figure 3.1, represents an electronic transmission. Because this fast-food restaurant still uses vocal sound methods for communication with the customer, we will use straight arrows for those actions and standard electronic symbols for a microphone and a speaker to represent the order taker. However, the zigzag arrow symbols are a better choice for some of the back-office communications with computer systems. These modifications are shown in Figure 3.5 along with the other modifications described later in the text.

At the beginning of the process, customers usually read the menu before making their choices of what to order. Since most fast-food restaurants display a static menu at the ordering station, we will represent that information with a document symbol from Figure 3.1 to indicate that it is on a physical medium.

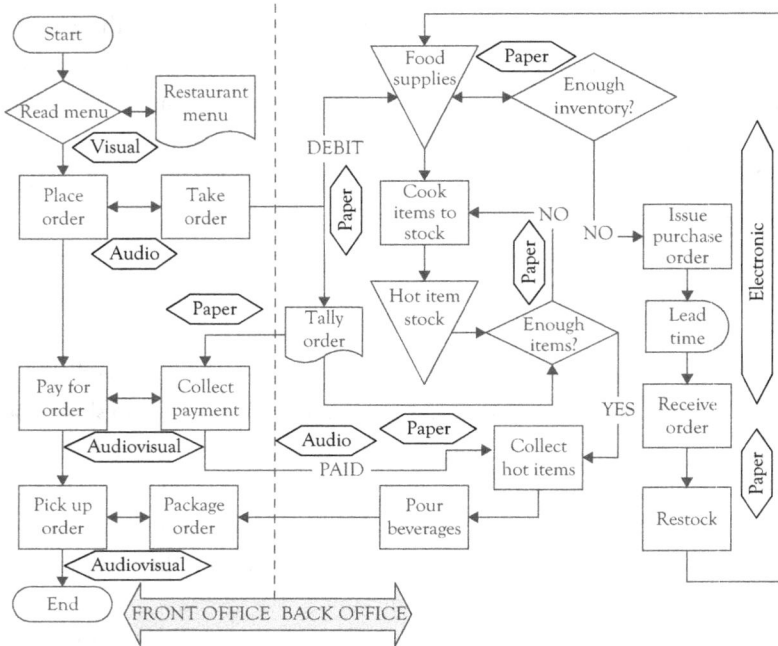

Figure 3.5. Service process blueprint from figure 3.3 modified to show the information process content more clearly.

Now consider the transfer of order information to the cashier collecting payments and the person assembling the order. We will assume that the list of ordered items is in the form of a paper order filled out by the order taker and show a document symbol as part of the transfer process. The order goes first to the cashier to determine what the customer owes in payment and then to the assembly person. We are now at a decision point for the assembly person. If all of the cooked order items are already completed and waiting under the heat lamp, the assembly person proceeds to assemble the order for the customer. If not, then the order is given to the kitchen staff for them to prepare the required items and then returned to the assembly person with the finished items when they are completed.

More than collecting money occurs at the cashier station. The process of entering the list of items on each order into the cash register to calculate the total payment offers the best opportunity to collect point-of-sale data and also to input inventory changes. Otherwise, the order data given to the assembly person would have to be passed on in paper form after the customers pick up their orders for manual processing.

Potential Process Improvements

A number of potential process improvements can be considered when reviewing a completed process diagram. They can be changes in how items are physically handled or by identifying steps that appear to not add any value for the customer *or the business*[6] and thus can be eliminated. In many cases, particularly for service processes, the biggest benefit can come from improving, altering, or replacing some or all of the information process components. A suggested checklist of questions to ask is:

- Can we dematerialize some of the information?
- Can we acquire it more efficiently?
- Can we track it more efficiently?
- Can we process or transfer it differently?
- Can we eliminate some duplication of information?
- Can we obtain additional useful information?
- Can customers do some of the above for us?

Because the emphasis here is on the value of integrating information process considerations with other business process considerations we will not discuss other improvement possibilities such as food preparation methods here. That will be left to a subsequent book focused on overall process analysis and improvement methods updated to include the integration of information processes. Given this constraint, let's address the above checklist as it applies to the fast-food restaurant customer ordering process.

The use of paper documents is still common to many smaller businesses and even parts of larger enterprises because it is easy to implement and familiar to employees. However, the ability to convert information conveyed on a physical medium such as paper into a digital form that can be processed electronically offers many benefits to business processes and should be the first thing to consider when improving a process currently dependent on paper documentation. Within a given process, the earlier in the process sequence that dematerialization is done, the greater the potential benefit. Here, a good choice would be for the order taker to enter the order information electronically using a traditional keyboard or a touch-screen display. By sending the information directly to the restaurant's main computer system for processing, the computer can calculate the amount owed and send it electronically to the cashier, make the decision as to whether or not a make-to-order request needs to be sent to the kitchen, store the POS data, record a reduction in inventory supplies created by the order, notify purchasing when more inventory is needed, and so forth.

Note that just dematerializing the information also helps answer several of the other questions on the checklist. They could be answered without eliminating the use of paper forms, but the answers would be constrained to less effective possibilities such as redesigning the order form for easier entry and having the cashier enter the POS data into the central computer instead of the order taker.

A hidden advantage for the restaurant using this order process improvement is that they can gain additional information about customer demand. As the order is now in a dematerialized form, the input system can easily add other data that might affect the order, such as time of day, day of the week, weather information, number of customers waiting in line, and so forth, to the order data. An example of the use of such data is given at the end of appendix C where we discuss an application using Excel's PivotTable function.

The last question on the checklist is perhaps the second-most important one for a service process improvement. Allowing customers to do some of the service helps businesses in a number of ways. It allows more standardization of the service process and reduces labor costs by having the customer perform some of the desired customization. An example is providing condiment stations so that customers can add what they want to their food or beverage instead of asking the restaurant staff to do it for them and increasing the complexity of the order information. Letting the inside customers pour their own beverages is another example and it gives them something to do while waiting in line for the rest of their order.

Using this approach, let's return to the ordering step and combine it with some advances in information technology to allow the customer to

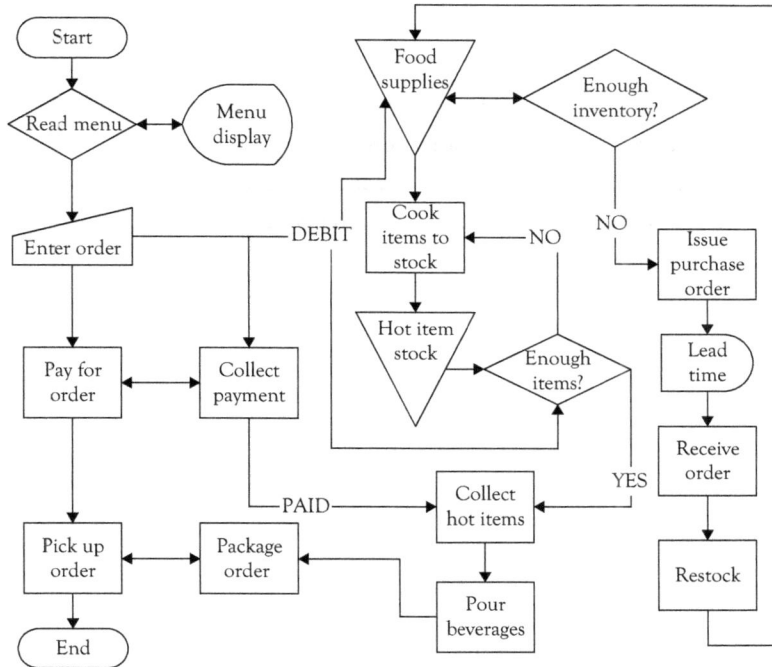

Figure 3.6. Customer order process step modified to take advantage of information processing technology to provide dematerialized order information.

dematerialize the order information as shown in Figure 3.6. The traditional menu is now a flat-screen display. Such displays have become larger, more reliable, and less expensive to the extent that they now can be used by fast-food restaurants to display their menu choices. Besides the high-tech look, such displays have the advantage of being easily updated to include seasonal promotions on the menu or to remove items temporarily out of stock. Animation sequences are also possible to help promote different items on the menus. A separate smaller display with a keypad or touch-screen capability is used by the customer to enter their order by either entering a code displayed with each item on the menu, or touching a corresponding button on the touch-screen. When the customer is ready to submit their order, it is summarized on the screen for their verification before they do so. This not only enters the order information in a dematerialized form at the earliest point in the process, but also eliminates the need for an order taker and the possible communication errors between the order taker and the customer.

A few years ago, these improvements would have also required some customer education and familiarization to use the order entry process correctly. With the widespread use of ATMs and online shopping order entry, the new customer ordering steps should be familiar to most customers.

CHAPTER 4

Use and Acquisition of Information

We will begin this chapter with an aerial view of how information may be used by a business, then spend some time discussing specific details about uses in different functions, followed by some methods for acquiring information more easily and with less cost, and conclude with some suggestions for reducing the effort required to handle information in manufacturing and inventory applications.

Many of you should already be familiar with the B2B, B2C, C2B, and C2C terminology describing the four basic e-commerce interactions between businesses and customers where the first letter represents the creator or supplier of data and products and the second letter represents the receiver or user of data and products. For those of you who are not, Figure 4.1 should bring you up-to-date with a few examples of e-commerce businesses whose product or service is best described by each interaction.

Figure 4.2 adds some new interactions to support the growing presence of Big Data applications, Internet-of-Things (IoTs) concepts, the effect of social media, and the increased use of the Internet for interactions between the governments and their citizens and businesses. This has expanded the role of the Internet from that of being a primary communication link between businesses and customers to also becoming an independent information source and a method of direct communication between various types of equipment. The types of interactions have also increased in complexity.

The term customer normally describes an individual who has a direct financial relationship (money changes hands), that is, acts as either an individual buyer or a seller. Sometimes, however, a customer has only an influential or informative role in the interaction, for example, when the customer is responding to a survey sent out by a business, posting a review

	Business	Customer
Business	B2B Supply chain transactions, services subcontracting	B2C e-tailers, catalogs, product information & training
Customer	C2B Price negotiations, product buybacks, warranty claims	C2C Online auctions, online classified ads, product reviews

Figure 4.1. Interaction matrix for businesses and customers. The use of the Internet as a communication path is assumed in all cases.

	Business	Customer	Government	Machine	Internet
Business	B2B	B2C	B2G	B2M	B2I
Customer	C2B	C2C	C2G	C2M	C2I
Government	G2B	G2C	G2G	G2M	G2I
Machine	M2B	M2C	M2G	M2M	M2I
Internet	I2B	I2C	I2G	I2M	N/A

Figure 4.2. Interaction matrix for businesses, customers/citizens, governments, machines, and the Internet. The role of the Internet as a communication path is assumed in all cases. Note that since the Internet is considered to be a single entity, describing interactions with itself is not applicable here.

regarding a product on an e-tailer's website, or seeking technical support. Another growing type of online interaction involving individuals is the interaction between citizens and their government. Today, a number of governments have increased their presence on the web by encouraging citizens to submit applications and make payments for licenses, sign-up for governmental benefits, buy postage, and file their taxes electronically. In Figure 4.2, these types of relationships are still represented by the customary C for a customer (or citizen), but it is still important to recognize their differences.

The increased number and complexity of the interactions that now take place using the Internet is another illustration of the increasing growth on information.

Classes of Interactions

Defining each of the 24 interactions shown in Figure 4.2 separately would take more time and space than is appropriate for this monograph. Hence, we will summarize them according to the viewpoint of the primary sender or initiator of the communication in an interaction, recognizing that most interactions are necessarily two-way exchanges.

Business

As more and more information became dematerialized in the past decade, business-to-business interactions primarily moved online to support the growing need to exchange information with suppliers, warehouses, and retailers quickly. This includes sales to other businesses in a supply chain.

While many purchases, particularly material items needed quickly (food, beverages, and gasoline), are still sold to customers in brick-and-mortar stores, the percentage of total sales done online and sent directly to customers continues to increase. This trend requires businesses to review frequently how they collect point-of-sale data, market their product, communicate with customers, and handle warranty and quality issues. Of particular concern to traditional brick-and-mortar retailers is the growing practice often referred to as "show rooming," where a customer checks out a product in their store and then buys it online from another retailer for a lower price. Easy price comparisons made possible by advances in cell phone technology such as the ability to scan product barcodes are another disturbing trend for such retailers.

The use of the Internet by a business to communicate with a machine is relatively new, but it allows some considerable advantages because communication with such equipment is considerably simpler and can use display and analysis capability that is already in place. This allows remote control and monitoring of manufacturing equipment, security systems, and faster acquisition of information from a variety of sensors.

As the number of Internet users has grown, more businesses are using the Internet for advertising, catalogs, posting product information and manuals, training, and generic technical support (support for a specific customer's problem is a B2C interaction). The practice of moving from printed manuals and guidebooks to e-books and other downloadable files dematerializes these information products for more rapid and flexible distribution and eliminates printing, stocking, shipping, and revision costs.

Customer

Customers and citizens are, in my mind, the biggest beneficiaries of online communications. Never before in the history of mankind has an individual had the ability to access so much information easily and quickly. The development of easy-to-use and intelligent search engines and the increasing availability of social media sites, blogs, and online education courses covering a wide range of interests allow anyone with a web connection to acquire information from around the world. I am particularly amazed at the range of video content posted by individuals that provides do-it-yourself (DIY) information,[1] musical performances, lectures by leading scientists and scholars, tours of scenic sites and historical monuments, and so forth. As discussed in the previous paragraph, businesses are now learning the value of joining this information-sharing environment, not only to reduce the costs of providing product information but also as a new advertising medium.

The classic example of the C2B interaction in many business textbooks is a customer negotiating with a business regarding the price that the customer is willing to pay for that business's product offering, most commonly a hotel room or a similar perishable product such as an airplane seat, entertainment event, or a Christmas tree still on the sales lot the day before Christmas. But, given the ease of online access and more immediate response, more customers are also contacting business websites for product information or training, to submit product reviews, ask for technical help, or process warranty claims. In some instances, individuals act as temporary sellers to business. Some examples are selling textbooks back to online book dealers or selling used electronic devices to businesses that refurbish for them for resale in other countries.

Government

Ironically, governmental agencies were the primary users in the early days of what evolved into the Internet. Their presence became secondary during the dot-com growth in the 1990s and then expanded later. Today, many governments are increasingly using the Internet as the primary means for communicating with their citizens and conducting business with them. Electronic filing of tax returns speeds up revenue collection and reduces processing costs. Similar savings and reductions in response time are possible for other activities such as benefits claims for veterans and seniors, provided such agencies update their processes to dematerialize their paper information and enable them to take advantage of the advances in information technology. Governments can also use Internet connectivity to acquire weather and traffic information from monitoring equipment, perform surveillance, activate warning systems, and so forth.

The challenges here are how to handle two significantly different types of users—those who are familiar with using the Internet and those who are not, often older citizens who frequently have a greater need to communicate with governmental agencies. Another complication is providing equal access for all of a country's citizens. Many rural areas in even developed countries currently have no broadband access, limited Internet capability, or none at all. This is also a problem for small and medium businesses operating in such areas.

Machine

The idea of connecting machines to computers for data acquisition and control applications is far from new as we described in the history segment of chapter 1. What is new is the ability to connect machines with computers in two or more locations anywhere in the world without using hardwired interfaces. The use of cell phone networks and the Internet allows equipment and sensors in one location to communicate easily with other sensors and equipment in other locations, enabling the use of multiple automatic monitoring systems and the coordination of activities among facilities. This also allows equipment to contact customers or businesses directly to notify them of a changed condition or other event of interest. Many machines can now be programmed remotely over the Internet. The variety of applications made possible by this connectivity, often referred to as the Internet of Things (IoTs), has exploded in recent years. Some more familiar examples, besides the obvious security monitoring applications, are programming your DVR at home to record a favorite TV show while you are still traveling, weather and traffic webcams located in many cities, webcams monitoring baby owls in a nest for scientific study by naturalists and entertainment for the public, sensors monitoring the structural integrity of the new interstate highway bridge in Minnesota, and children checking on the daily health of their aged parents living some distance away. While the real usefulness of the solution is yet to be determined, there are even refrigerators that monitor their content and notify their owners via the Internet when to pick up some more milk or eggs on their way home.

We will talk more about these types of applications later in this chapter and subsequent chapters because they can offer inexpensive capabilities to SMBs and their requirements must be considered when selecting external software and infrastructure solutions.

Internet

We normally do not think of the Internet initiating an interaction on its own, but many businesses have developed applications that ask it to do exactly that. To clarify what I mean, I am not referring to the product suggestions relative to your interests that pop up on an e-tailer's website when you are viewing it with the intention of ordering something else. That is more correctly described as a B2C interaction with a frequent customer. Instead, the Internet information sites often act as the primary intermediary for a collection of businesses much like old-time print newspapers did. While some would call it acting as a general advertising medium, the difference is that the Internet can target that advertising on an individual basis using the reader's location (GPS coordinates, zip code, or IP address) and previous browsing history. In addition, the Internet has communication advantages that print media does not have, such as sound, video, animation, and the ability to download information in both electronic and print forms.

The businesses do not know who each customer is until that customer chooses to contact them in response to an advertisement—a C2B interaction after a B2I—I2C set of interactions. Keep in mind here that the potential customer went on the Internet to read the news, not scan advertisements for stuff the customer might be interested in buying. If a customer wants to buy an item, the customer will either go directly to a trusted e-tailer they think has what they want or they will use a search engine to find one. Clicking on a pop-up advertisement is generally not wise unless one recognizes the advertiser and has a strong antivirus and malware detection program monitoring their Internet connections.

Acquiring Information

How we do this is governed by our current level of understanding and some basic measurement rules. That is, you cannot measure or assign attributes to something when you are unaware of its existence. Likewise, if you are aware of the existence of something, but you and other people who are also aware of it cannot agree on how to measure or describe it, sharing what understanding you have is very difficult. These situations occur more often in business situations than one would expect. A common example is a product failure or a poor service result that occurs occasionally for no discernible reason. To prevent them from happening in the future, you need to know the cause. However, until some piece of information is correlated with the undesired outcomes, you have no idea of where to begin your investigation. Big Data analysis methods can help find such correlations when you have accumulated large amounts of data, but you need to remember the fundamental rule "Conclusions are only as good as the information used to derive them." or more colorfully stated as GIGO, "garbage in, garbage out!" Acquiring large amounts of information can give businesses false confidence that they have enough to solve problems or gain deeper insight into how their businesses work. This also carries over into many of today's engineering design approaches where many experiments are run under a wide range of conditions to accumulate huge amounts of test data. The data are then analyzed to find correlations, probabilities, other relationships, and optimum sets of results to select the best design tried and perhaps identify what parameters to adjust for better performance.

In effect, they are playing a Battleship game against a small fleet of enemy ships in a very big ocean. The more experimental shots they fire, the quicker they can find the enemy fleet. But if they have limited supplies of ammunition, this is not an effective use of their resources. Consider, however, that they do some intelligence work first to determine what possible ports the enemy fleet could have left from and when. Then making an estimate of the fleet's speed from those possible locations could help narrow the area of the ocean for their barrages of shots considerably.

There are two important lessons to learn here. The first lesson is that data-mining methods work with known parameters; they are very poor at finding unknown parameters other than maybe indicating that some may exist because no significant correlations are found in a data set. Sometimes you can identify some conditions that your experience tells you are relatively sure to affect your desired results, but you just cannot figure out yet how to measure them. This is an opportunity to gain a competitive advantage if you can. Some useful references in this regard are the book on business measurements by Hubbard[2] and chapter 5 on seeking for a pattern in noise, from the book by Silver.[3]

The second lesson is that collecting, storing, and analyzing data is a significant business expense, both in support costs and in diversions of employee time and attention away from the core processes of the business. Occasionally, spend some time to review what information your business really needs and what information is proving to be not worth the cost of acquiring it. Integrating the use of information with other process improvements as discussed in chapter 3 is an effective way of doing such a review.

Some Suggestions for Data Acquisition

There are many ways a business can acquire data. The trick, of course, is to use methods that are inexpensive and provide information most relevant to a particular business. Data acquisition processes that are an integrated part of other business processes are the best choice, particularly those daily operations processes required for producing the services or products a business offers to its customers. Some suggestions for sources of useful information are:

- POS (point-of-sale) data.
- Customer support data.
- Performance data.
- Time data.
- Monitoring data.

- GPS (global positioning system) data.
- Frequency data.
- External data.

POS data are high-yielding ore for data mining. In addition to its original primary value of providing information for business accounting processes, it is the optimum source for acquiring all sorts of information regarding customer behavior and preferences. By choosing the appropriate format, POS data can also provide information directly to inventory management, staff scheduling, and marketing functions. With some innovation and careful design of customer ordering, shipping, and payment processes, a business can obtain greater informational content at its POSs at a minimal cost. In some cases, a business can even get their customers to do most of the input. One example of how to do this was described in chapter 3, Figure 3.6. Other common examples are the online ordering processes used by many e-tailers.

Data Input Considerations

We should digress a bit here to discuss how important the data input process design is when customers are asked to input data for use by a business.

Customer spelling errors, wide choice of word answers, misinterpretation of form instructions, and so forth, are the major contributors to errors in business databases, duplication of entries, and an overall increase in the complexity of the data. Using dropdown lists of acceptable answers, asking customers to verify critical data by entering it twice for comparison, restricting their unstructured input to text boxes, and making a strong effort to ensure the instructions are correctly understood can prevent many problems and enhance the value of the information provided. We will return to discussing further the importance of such activity in chapter 6.

In effect, one could say that data sources directly or indirectly related to customers are "front office" sources and data sources from internal business activities are "back office" sources where more control over the content and veracity of the data is possible. This is not to imply that internal data are always more structured and accurate. It is not unusual in a company with well-designed customer input processes to find functions and employees not following the same regimen when they are entering internal performance information. This is particularly troublesome for upper-level managers and IT organizations when those functions and employees are maintaining local databases in addition to the company's central database.

Customer Support Data

Customer support data are particularly useful for preventing future problems and obtaining information for directing efforts to improve products and production processes. These data should include customer returns and warranty claims. There are several advantages in combining these processes with other customer requests for help and information as part of a business's website. The information is obtained in an easily processed dematerialized form, the customer does most of the work to enter it into a company's database, and the response to a customer's concerns is more readily available.

Performance Data

Most businesses collect some data about how well their more important processes are performing, usually with regard to cost, throughput, yield, downtime or uptime, and utilization or capacity. In large enterprise companies that can afford to use automated processes, a significant amount of these data is relatively easy to acquire. In many SMBs, most of these data are manually acquired and summarized by managers or senior staff at the end of a shift, day, or other reporting period most suitable for a particular business.

While useful for planning, accounting, scheduling, and monitoring purposes, these data are often inadequate for use in preventing problems, resolving problems quickly when they do occur, or for identifying more specific areas for process improvements. What is often missing is adequate time information. Just knowing exactly when different activities in each functional area are occurring and which person, machine, or information system is performing them at that time can be of significant help. This enables easier identification of trends for use in preventative action decisions and maintenance. The ability to correlate events across more than one company function or department helps quickly identify less obvious causes of process failures, such as a change in a material supplier or a modification of a support process. Most of this information can be added simply and inexpensively in dematerialized information systems by including their internal timestamps and identifiers in the data set.[4]

Monitoring Data

Monitoring information is a necessity in some businesses, particularly those handling food items, providing security systems, growing plants in greenhouses, supplying utilities such as electricity and natural gas, refining oil, or running any other operation where proper environmental conditions are critical to their success or safety. Monitoring such data in the past allowed us to respond quickly to an undesirable condition. It also was necessary to provide documentation to regulators that we had complied with the necessary requirements to ensure that our customers received a safe-to-use product. Many of these systems were either primarily mechanical or electrical in nature. Some of the monitoring devices allowed a possibility of recording their measurements versus time on paper, such as the circular temperature or pressure chart recorders that some older manufacturing workers are likely to be familiar with. However, many of them required manual reading and recording at specified time intervals, a process that was subject to errors in entering both measured values and the times they were taken.

Thanks to advances in measurement and information technologies, an increasing majority of such monitoring needs can now be recorded directly in electronic form. Such records not only satisfy the safety and regulatory requirements, but the data now can also be processed in real time to predict the possibility of an unsafe or other undesired condition early enough to prevent it from happening. Many of the preventive maintenance software solutions now available depend on such monitoring data.

GPS Data

The ability to output location information directly in digital formats has not only made navigation much easier, but has also enabled the easy use of location information for controlling processes, analyzing potential markets, targeting more appropriate advertising, and directly labeling images with their location. As a result, correlating data to locations has become an important business tool. This is especially evident in many decision support systems and logistics strategies. The expanding use of GPS data not only for internal business use but also for services and products such as enhanced mapping applications, survey equipment, and personal navigation systems has created a subdiscipline in the IT community called GIS (Geographical Information Systems).

The rapidly growing use of smartphones worldwide[5] has created a corresponding growth in targeted advertising and other services based on location data. One common example is displaying nearby businesses on a person's smartphone in reply to their search for a place to eat or stay or as part of a query about prices and nearby stores for something they want to buy.

Frequency Data

While it can be argued that frequency information is really part of the data sets we have already discussed, it deserves separate attention because of its importance in evaluating risks and making yield management choices. Most businesses have to cope with demand variations and external factors that are difficult to predict. For physical products with a reasonable shelf life, they can use a safety stock inventory strategy, but for products with a very limited shelf life or services offerings they need to anticipate these effects on their business as well as they can. One way to improve their chances of success is to improve their ability to predict what will happen next. Determining possible seasonal variations for customer demand and the probability distributions for the occurrences of external factors that might affect that demand or the business's performance is usually a good place to start.

Consider a simple yield management problem where you own a hotel. If you do not have enough reservations by the time the rooms should be occupied, you lose money on the empty rooms. The incremental overhead expense for servicing each room must now be recovered with less revenue. The situation is the same for empty seats on an airplane flight. The common solution for such a problem is to begin offering discounts or other incentives to bring in more customers to occupy the unreserved rooms or fill the empty seats before takeoff. A common complication is that some of the reservations are likely to be cancelled at the last minute.

To cope with these last-minute cancellations where there is little time left for offering incentives and discounts, many hotels and airlines overbook their capacity when the demand is high by the number of customers they think will cancel at the last minute. Where do they get this number? Furthermore, what happens if they overbook too much? How do they handle the customers who must be turned away? What's the probability of that happening?

This is why collecting frequency data is important. By counting the number of times in a given period (a time long enough to include all or at least most of the possible values) there were no cancellations, just one cancellation, just two cancellations, and so on, one can calculate the probability of each cancellation level by dividing the number of times it occurred by the total number of nights or plane flights covered by the period. If one is lucky, the resulting range of discrete probabilities may correlate closely enough to a standard probability distribution such as Poisson, normal, or binominal that the mathematical function describing the distribution can be used in future calculations regarding the best choice for an overbooking level. If not, then the set of discrete probability values can be used directly to determine the optimum overbooking level. In a similar fashion, frequency data regarding sales volumes for perishable items can help a retailer determine the optimum number to stock of each item.

Of more general interest to businesses is the value of frequency data to identify seasonal factors for more accurate forecasts of demand. The granularity of such data will vary, of course, from business to business depending on the nature of the business and the intended use of the data. For example, staff scheduling will likely require daily or weekly values and production of make-to-stock items may only need monthly or quarterly values. Such decisions regarding the collection of frequency data and the desired level of detail are critical for success when a business decides to incorporate the use of an enterprise software solution.

To do this using internal POS data and other information collected from past events, that information needs to include whether or not some of the external factors occurred at each event and more specifically which ones. Then, for some defined levels of performance such as lost money, broke even, made money, or really cleaned up, count the number of times each level of performance occurred for each combination of demand and possible factors. Then, by dividing the total number of times you lost money for a given combination by the total number of times you encountered that combination, you can obtain a rough estimate of the probability of losing money if you encounter that combination in the future.

For example, consider that your business is providing snack foods and beverages for outside events. The number of expected customers can vary for a number of reasons—the popularity of the event, the weather, other events at the same time, current economic conditions, and so forth. The types of snacks and beverages the customers would expect to be offered can also be affected by the nature of the event, the weather, economic conditions, and so forth. So, how would you choose what types of food and beverages to bring to an outdoor event when the weather forecast says there is a strong probability it will be rainy and cold? What quantity of each chosen food and beverage item should you buy in order to obtain the best return and satisfy your customers well enough that they would want to do business with you again?

One answer is to just give such choices your best guess based on what you can remember from the past experiences. A better strategy is to add some information to your business's POS data when it is collected. The normal sales receipts provide enough demand data to answer questions about product mixes, but it will not explain, for example, that the reason hot coffee purchases were greater at some events than others is that the number of such purchases is typically higher on a cooler day or when it is raining. While you can add such information to future POS data, what about the large amount of past POS data collected by your business? This is where clever use of external data available from other sources and Big Data concepts can help give you a competitive advantage over other event providers.

External Data

The first seven suggestions relate to information that is best collected internally by a business to best capture the nuances in such data that are characteristic of that particular business. To supplement internal data to answer questions posed in the previous two paragraphs, you need to consult some of the many external sources available. Some are free such as US census data available online at http://www.census.gov/#, data from the European Union online at http://europa.eu/index_en.htm, and data from many other US government agencies online at http://www.usa.gov/Topics/Reference-Shelf/Data.shtml and http://www.data.gov/. An easy web search looking for information about other countries can direct you to a number of governmentally supported websites that not only tell you about their country and its government, but also provide useful business data regarding transportation capabilities, customs regulations, their primary business strengths, and so forth.

A number of businesses provide information for other businesses as their primary product. Marketing firms can do customer preference and satisfaction surveys or evaluate the effectiveness of a business's advertising among their other capabilities. In the United States, a relatively inexpensive reference that has been useful for SMBs in assessing market potential, location considerations, transportation networks available, and other start-up or expansion information is a commercial atlas such as the one published by Rand McNally.[6]

Two of the most significant sources available regarding customer preferences are the databases accumulated by online search engine and social network providers. Their databases are a result of the ultimate use of customers inputting information regarding their interests, preferences, dislikes, what they have questions about, referrals to other potential customers, and in many cases their personal contact and location information in real time. While many of the individual data inputters are not yet fully aware of the extent of the data they are entering, some are beginning to express concerns about the privacy of some of their information in social network applications. Such concerns also apply to SMBs that use these applications for communication with their customers. We will discuss these concerns further in chapter 6.

External data sources are especially useful for start-up businesses needing background data for their business plans. Because they obviously will not have accumulated much internal data yet, reviewing appropriate data already collected by other representative businesses can be useful when setting up their internal processes. Such data for more common processes are often available in local small business support organizations.

During the pursuit of better ways to handle information in traditional business processes a number of new ways to do business more effectively have been discovered and turned into practice. Some of the more fortuitous examples are included as part of the following discussion on ways to handle information to provide readers a starting point for possibly adapting them to their particular business situation.

Methods of Handling of Information

Considerable effort is spent by businesses to input and otherwise handle the information they need for decisions, process instructions, and record keeping for a variety of accounting, tax reporting, and regulatory requirements. The information for businesses involved in supplying services such as medical examinations, haircuts, lawn care, tax preparation, house painting, and other offerings that do not require tracking of completed physical inventory[7] has become more automated with either direct computer entry by the employees performing the service or by the customers requesting it. But, for many back office activities supporting those services and for businesses producing, distributing, storing, and selling physical products, there is still a need to physically track the status and whereabouts of those products and easily link that information to other business processes like inventory management, procurement, pricing, and POS systems.

A plethora of books, articles, and other references exists regarding how to best handle information for most common business processes. Here we concentrate on more recent technological advances in information handling applications for manufacturing, retail, and customer interactions with the observation that many of the advances in these areas are now being applied to other processes such as record keeping, tracking workflows, and providing information to employees and supply chain partners more quickly. Some of these advances that have made material handling and related information processing much more efficient, less expensive, and more accurate are:

- Optical barcode labeling and scanning technology
- Development of standard codes for different business segments
  - Universal product code (UPC)
  - International standard book number (ISBN)
  - Postal codes (ZIP code in USA)
  - QR (quick response) code
- RFID (radio frequency identification) technology
- Optical character recognition (OCR)
- GPS technology

Barcode

The use of barcodes is now ubiquitous in modern societies primarily because they reduce the time required to enter information accurately. In addition, that information is in a dematerialized form that can be readily processed, stored, copied, and transferred. Some examples of commonly used barcodes are shown later in this chapter along with a discussion regarding how the coding works and associated applications.

This technology had its beginnings in the late 1940s and early 1950s when a food chain president expressed an interest at the Drexel Institute of Technology regarding having an automated system developed for reading grocery items at the checkout station. In response, two graduate students at Drexel developed a method using a code consisting of alternating lines of varying widths configured in both circular and line patterns and read with an electronic device also of their design. Their invention was submitted for a patent in 1949 and it was approved in late 1952.[8]

However, their reading method required a very bright incandescent bulb and physical movement of either the detector or the code. In addition, it required the development of a sufficient number of unique code patterns to represent the various grocery items for it to be practical. This could have been done on a store-by-store basis with each food chain developing its own code, printing it on adhesive labels and affixing them to the respective product in their inventory. But the remaining roadblock was the scanning system: the bulb emitted a lot of heat, the scan was slow, and the overall size was much larger than a cash register. It required advances in electronics from vacuum tubes to transistors, the development of the laser, agreements by several different food chains and their suppliers on a standardized code for grocery items, and the development of some internal barcode applications by some major industries before the first grocery store installations occurred in 1973.

At first, the technology only provided a list of the items selected by a customer, although it certainly was faster than the cashier entering the list manually. Prices still needed to be entered separately. Stock boys at that time had to stick two labels on grocery products, one label for the code, and another label for the price. Later, the labels were improved to have both the code and the price on the same label and food manufacturers began printing the codes for their products on the cartons, cans, and bottles they came in.

Transportation industries began using barcodes to track their rolling stock such as rail cars, semi-trailers, and large shipping containers. However, because the reading distances were greater and the environments dirtier, such labels were often misread or were not readable at all. Some of these industries such as railroad companies changed to using RFID devices for this tracking.[9] RFID devices were more expensive, but they were not discarded after use like the grocery store barcode labels; instead, they could be used a long time and their reliability was much better.

The advances in computer technology and decreasing cost of standalone computer systems combined with greatly enhanced barcode standards around the globe provided much more capability for all businesses to cut their material handling costs and increase productivity. Now the readers could not only provide the cashier with a quick list of the items to be purchased, but also the computer in the checkout station could correlate each item's barcode with its current price in the inventory database, debit the inventory stock for that item, add up the total cost for the customer, calculate correct change, and print out time and day on the receipt. This also eliminated the need for stock boys to attach new price labels to existing stock when the price changed for a sale. But the cashier still had to manually handle each item to pass it over the scanner, enter the data by hand for smudged or missing barcodes, collect payment, handout any change, and bag up the items. Today, self-service checkout lines with automated payment capability allow the customer to do most of the manual activity with cashier assistance only needed for smudged or missing barcodes.

Another advantage is that a business or an individual customer can easily print their own barcode labels using equipment already available in businesses and households capable of using the Internet. This ability was important in the early days of the technology when manufacturers had not yet established the practice of printing bar-coded information on their packaging. Today it is used by consumers to print their own boarding passes for expedited check-in at airports, tickets for events that they have purchased online, and so forth. An application useful for SMBs is printing a custom menu of barcodes for employees to use when inputting inspection data, machine settings for a particular process, specialized conditions at checkout stations, customer complaints, or other defined sets of information used by the business.

A new application is the use of smartphone cameras for reading product barcodes. This allows users to check on a price for an item before reaching the checkout station and even compare it with the price offered at another store.

Like most things in life, there are some disadvantages to consider in using barcodes for data input. Some of them are as follows:

- Scanning requirements
  - Visibility
  - Clarity
  - Distance
  - Orientation
- Scanning time
- Limited data
- Inflexibility

The biggest disadvantage and one that is hard to overcome is the barcode has to be visible in its entirety to read it correctly. This means no significant smudges or wrinkles and the package carrying the barcode has to be positioned so the scanner can see all of the barcode. Coupled with this requirement is the maximum distance from the scanner which is usually less than a few inches. In some industrial applications, a lens-and-camera system can be used to acquire an image of a barcode from a greater distance and that image can be analyzed by a computer process to decode the information. However, this is not usually a practical solution for many barcode applications.

At one time, the orientation of the barcode relative to the scanner was much more critical for a correct reading. Advances in how the laser beam is scanned in different directions across a barcode have eliminated this disadvantage in more recent scanner versions.

Another disadvantage is that the time required to scan a group of items is still controlled by the time to orient and scan each item. Shipping departments in large warehouses, express mail operations, and airport baggage-handling systems reduce this time as much as possible by specifying where to place the shipping label with the bar-coded information on a package and then to put the package on the sorting conveyor belt with the label facing up or to one side, depending on where the sorting system mounts its barcode scanners. Similarly, it is important for a warehouse to have a policy regarding initial placement of items on shelves so that their barcodes can be easily scanned without the need for rearranging the items to do so.

Many of the standard codes only provide identification information such as the manufacturer, the country of origin, and a product identifier. If a manufacturer wants to track other information such as product versions, date of manufacture, and expiration dates, additional custom-designed barcode labels are required along with requirements for their placement relative to the standard identification label.

Finally, barcodes cannot be changed once printed. This disadvantage can be partly offset by the practice of associating the relatively simple code on the label with more easily modified information in a company's database such as the latest price of the item or its description. It becomes awkward when the same standard identification barcode in a warehouse inventory represents both older and newer versions of a product using this approach.

Figure 4.3. Examples of some commonly used barcode standards:
(a) UPC, (b) ISBN, (c) POSTNET (top) and Intelligent Mail
(bottom), and (d) QR codes for the ISBN of the author's earlier
book on waiting lines (left) and the URL regarding this book
on the publisher's website (right).

Development of Barcode Standards

The use of barcodes in processes related to consumers or external suppliers
requires some form of standardization so that all of the participants are able
to access and share the same information. Some examples of common barcode standards are shown in Figure 4.3.

While barcodes used only for internal operations can be any code the
business wants to develop, it is best to keep that code as close as possible to
standard formats in order to take advantage of commercially available scanning solutions. To clarify this statement, the UPC barcode standard spe-
cifies what each of the numbers of the code can represent when a merchant
prints a UPC code on their product. Okay, some of you already familiar
with the UPC code are likely to say, "Wait a minute! Each manufacturer is
responsible for at least part of the UPC code, what about that?" (We will go
into more detail about this later). In any case, when the UPC format is used

only for an internal business need, those numbers can be used to represent anything the business wants. A part of the UPC standard supports such internal applications by using one value for the first number to indicate that the following numbers do not correspond to any values in the standard UPC database. Some common internal uses for the UPC format are part numbers, filing labels, lab test requests, and so forth. This allows the business to use a standard barcode reader to scan the code internally with the results correlated to the business's internal database instead of the standard UPC database.

The UPC standard uses 12 digits to represent the country of origin, the manufacturer, a description of the product, and a check digit. The actual values represented by the various lines and spaces in the machine-readable pattern are printed at the bottom so that a human can read and enter the data if the pattern is too smudged or otherwise damaged for an accurate scan.

When a manufacturer applies to the Uniform Code Council (UCC) for registration of its products, the UCC uses the first six digits to assign an ID number to that manufacturer. The first digit is used to indicate particular classifications like random-weight items (2), pharmaceuticals (3), in-house use (4), and coupons (5). A particular useful classification (0) is used for abbreviated UPC labels to indicate that the code contains suppressed (not shown) zeros in the number sequence. This allows the use of UPC information on products with limited space for labels, such as beverage cans and bottles.

The next five digits are used for the item number and their assignment is the responsibility of the manufacturer in answer to the possible reader question given earlier. The last digit is a check digit that is used by the scanner to verify its accuracy in scanning the first 11 digits. Readers interested in more details about the UPC code and how it works are referred to a useful online reference by Brain.[10]

International Standard Book Number (ISBN) was developed initially as a 9-digit number more than 30 years ago by a statistics professor[11] at Trinity College in Dublin, Ireland, to simplify the identification of books for libraries and book retailers. Its value to the information processes used in this business segment increased its use to other countries, and it has been an international standard for identifying books and their publishers.

Today, each country has its own ISBN agency for assigning numbers to books published in that country. Earlier, ten digits were used to represent the book information. On January 1, 2007, the ISBN was expanded to 13 digits to handle the growing publication volume. Older 10-digit ISBNs are still in use, but can be converted to the 13-digit format by using a calculator on the ISBN agency's website at www.isbn.org. The agency emphasizes that an ISBN is not a barcode; it is the identification for a book. That said, these numbers are easily coded into an optically scanned format using the same methods as for UPC labels and are generally printed together with the ISBN on the book cover for easier data entry and tracking. Note: The barcode observed on the front of magazines and other periodicals is not an ISBN; UPC codes are typically used for these items. However, sometimes a special issue of a periodical will be sold as a book and it will have an ISBN assigned to it.

Books are identified by a 13-digit ISBN using five groups of information.

- The current three-digit prefix in the United States is "978"; this prefix will continue to be used until the entire set of book numbers available under that prefix is used up. At that time, the new prefix will be "979";
- This is followed by a group of one to five digits that identifies a national or geographic grouping of publishers;
- An identifier for a particular publisher within a group;
- An identifier for a particular title or edition of a title;
- A single check digit at the end of the ISBN, which validates the ISBN when it is scanned from a barcode format or transmitted electronically.

A new challenge is in deciding how the ISBN classification can be applied to electronic publications such as e-books. Because they are dematerialized information, there is no need for physical inventory tracking. Normal software file management solutions can handle distribution and storage needs. But, unlike most electronic files, there is a price associated with their distribution. So, how do we handle POS data for such transactions? Since an e-book is still a book, it would be simpler to use the same identification system as for other books.

Further complicating the situation is that an increasing percentage of the e-book publishers are individuals rather than the traditional big printing houses most of us are familiar with. An individual e-book author acting as one's own publisher can currently get an ISBN assigned to his or her book by applying to the agency in their country and paying an appropriate fee. But, given the explosive growth of e-publications, this ability is likely to undergo significant changes in the near future. Stay tuned!

The information processing and handling problems encountered in delivering mail and packages to the right address are an excellent example of the issues involved with handling primarily unstructured data. Just obtaining the correct city and state information is difficult when one considers customer spelling errors, bad handwriting, or printing. The US Postal Service began using codes to enable accurate sorting more quickly when they introduced the 5-digit Zip code to be used by their customers as the last entry in an address. The rules regarding what each digit in the Zip code represented were somewhat fuzzy at times, but, in general, the first three digits represented one of the numerous sorting centers distributed across the country. The last two digits represented one of the local post offices served by that center. This code added some structure to the address data and later could be read with acceptable accuracy by automated sorting equipment scanning POSTNET (Postal numerical encoding technique) barcodes representing the Zip code values. Unlike the lines and spaces with varying widths used in the UPC barcode, POSTNET uses combinations of five bars of two different heights to represent each number as shown in Table 4.1, variation similar to the dot–dash patterns used in Morse code.

Table 4.1. Bar coding for each numeral in a POSTNET barcode

Value	Encoding	Value	Encoding	Value	Encoding	Value	Encoding
1	ⅼⅼ‖	4	ⅼⅼⅼⅼ	7	‖ⅼⅼⅼ	0	‖ⅼⅼⅼ
2	ⅼⅼⅼⅼ	5	ⅼⅼⅼⅼ	8	ⅼⅼⅼⅼ		
3	ⅼⅼ‖ⅼ	6	ⅼⅼ‖ⅼ	9	ⅼⅼⅼⅼ		

An additional tall bar is used at each end to mark the start and ending of a POSTNET code.

The POSTNET format has had four versions over time to expand its coverage from a six-digit format for the original Zip code to its most recent version of 12 digits shown in Figure 4.3c representing the Zip+4 code plus the two last digits of the street address to allow further sorting of the mail at the receiving post office in order of delivery for the mail carrier. Version 4 is often referred as the Delivery Point Bar Code, or DPBC.

Implementation of the POSTNET code was not easy. While large-scale business users could be encouraged to use it for their mailing purposes by offering a discount if they did, individual users did not have the capability for printing POSTNET codes on their correspondence. Some word processing programs began offering the capability to their users, but a substantial amount of mail volume still did not have even a Zip code with the address. As a result, the post office began developing systems to print POSTNET codes on the submitted mail that did not have them and, as a result, was one of the first large-scale users of optical character recognition (OCR) technology in 1982, which we discuss in more detail later in this chapter. They used OCR to recognize typed or printed Zip codes in an address and then print the associated POSTNET code on the envelope for easier sorting as the mail moved through the distribution system. Handwritten address information still required manual reading by an operator to input the desired code to be printed on the envelope.

As the population has grown larger, the need for more information in the address code has resulted in the development of the USPS Intelligent Mail Barcode. This 31-digit barcode now uses four types of bars of different heights and ascending and descending portions instead of two different heights, as shown in Figure 4.3c, to provide more precise mailing information. Eventually, its use will be required to mail information at automated handling discount prices.

In the past decade, a new optically scanned code format developed in Japan in 1999 has come into use. Called QR for quick response and shown in Figure 4.3d, this code is two-dimensional with large targeting squares in three corners and a smaller square in the fourth corner to allow the optical reader, typically a smartphone or tablet computer camera, to orient the QR code for correct reading. The initial international standard for this new code, ISO/IEC 18004, was approved in June 2000, and later updated in 2006. I first encountered its use during a visit to Japan in 2005 where QR codes were displayed on billboards and other advertising on posters, train cars, and newspapers. Some even had simple pictures or graphics embedded in the code pattern to suggest the general nature of the information—a Mickey Mouse outline for a local Disney attraction, a bowl of noodles for a restaurant, and an octopus silhouette for a marine aquarium. The Japanese residents interested in the information just held up their smartphone to take a picture of the QR code; the smartphone then decoded the image and connected its owner to a website displaying further information or dialed a phone number for tickets or a reservation.

One QR code can contain up to 1,817 Kanji characters, 4,296 alphanumeric characters, or 7,089 numeric characters. To give you a better impression about what that capacity is, it is roughly equivalent to two pages of text from this book. In addition to the earlier advertising examples I observed in Japan, this capability could be used, for example, to display a menu of instructions for different work procedures on a single sheet of paper that could be quickly and accurately accessed by a machine operator and directly used to program a piece of equipment to machine a new part. It also means that a lawn tractor manufacturer could use just a few QR codes to print the entire user manual inside a cover panel or under the seat for the tractor, including servicing and trouble-shooting data, for easy access by the owner's smartphone or tablet computer. If additional help is needed, the QR codes could also provide the necessary information for accessing the manufacturer's website, for calling technical support, or to order a replacement part. Appropriate QR codes could also be printed on the back or front panels of home entertainment equipment, household appliances, and so forth, for the same purpose.

RFID

The idea of using radio waves to identify objects has been around much longer than optical barcode concepts. It can be said that the first radio frequency identification occurred when radar was invented. A radio pulse was sent out and was reflected back when an aircraft intercepted it. To be fair, the identification information was only that something was out there. When radio transmitters were added to friendly aircraft so that the transmitters could send back a coded reply indicating that they were a friend when interrogated by a radar pulse, the rudimentary concept of RFID technology was born.

The application of radio waves for more definitive identification was considered by a number of agencies during the 1950s and 1960s. One development was the idea of a single-bit device installed in a package or attached to a unit of merchandise. The device is turned on by the nature of its fabrication process for use in detecting someone leaving a building with the package or item without paying. After payment, it is deactivated, destroying it for further use. This initial passive design is still in use today for verifying tickets to events and for preventing theft of items from an exhibit. These devices are essentially a tiny radio antenna that is tuned to the frequency of the interrogating transceiver. Connecting the two halves (poles) of the antenna is a tiny capacitive diode. When a radio pulse of the proper frequency at a close range strikes the RFID device, it reflects that pulse back, sometime modifying that frequency slightly depending on the design of its antenna. It can be deactivated by subjecting it to a strong electromagnetic field like that used to demagnetize old cassette tapes, causing the tiny capacitive diode to overheat and burn out, much like an overloaded electrical fuse.

There are two basic types of RFID tags: passive and active. Each type has a range of similar capabilities for storing and transmitting information depending on the complexity the microchip used. Passive RFID devices have no internal energy source, such as a battery, making them much less expensive but not as cheap as a barcode label, which is also a passive device. Hence, their operation depends on the energy transmitted by the interrogation pulse from the radio transceiver attempting to read them. When these devices receive an interrogation pulse from the transceiver attempting to read them, the minute amount of energy in the pulse is used to power the small microchip in the device long enough for it to respond with the necessary information. This response is typically accomplished by the microchip acting as a variable capacitor to modulate the reflected part of the interrogation pulse in simpler passive devices. More sophisticated versions can send more information using a set of interrogation pulses that not only supply enough energy for the device to operate, but also instruct the device as to what information is wanted. In batch reading applications, the instruction set usually includes one telling the device not to reply to any further interrogation after the reader has obtained the information it wants for the moment.

Active RFID devices have their own energy source in the form of a battery or solar cell. This allows them to broadcast their information independently at programmed intervals, acting like a location beacon,[12] or enables them to perform more complex information storage and processing applications. These capabilities come at a higher per tag cost and, as a result, these tags are not typically used for routine retail or inventory tracking applications unless the items of interest are expensive or require substantial amounts of information or both for their management or maintenance.

At the current state of the art, simple passive RFID tags are still more expensive on a per tag cost basis than their barcode counterparts. From a strict IT perspective, this added cost has precluded their use in many retail and inventory management applications. But, when viewed from a more integrated information and process management viewpoint, the overall cost to a business is likely to be less because of the added process capabilities and efficiencies provided by RFID technology.

Let's compare some of these capabilities against the disadvantages of barcode applications. First, the scanning requirements are much more flexible. A line-of-sight view between an RFID tag and a radio transceiver used to read it is no longer necessary and orientation is not important. In fact, the tag can be out of sight inside a package container or beneath a pile of other items. While the communication between RFID tags and transceivers operating on UHF bands can be obscured by metals and liquids, this is largely not a problem for RFID systems operating at higher and lower radio frequencies. An RFID tag does not have to be in as close proximity to its reader compared to a barcode; typical scanning distances can range from one to two meters for smaller passive devices to more than several hundred meters for active devices.

If the RFID tag is an active device, it can even initiate the communication with readers based on some internally programmed schedule, something not possible with optically read barcodes. Some places where this capability is useful is tracking transportation equipment or notifying the maintenance department in a factory when a piece of equipment requires routine maintenance or calibration.[13] The tracking readers could also reply to tag the current location of the reader so that the tag itself could contain a history of where it has been.

A unique capability provided by not needing line-of-sight access to an item is finding specific items much more quickly. Imagine that your inventory shows that your business has an item in its warehouse that is needed quickly by a customer, but your warehouse supervisor cannot remember where it is physically located since it was purchased some time ago. A bar-coded inventory would require an item-by-item search to find it. By setting an RFID reader to the desired part number in an RFID tagged inventory, the supervisor only has to scan each section of the warehouse for a minute or so to quickly find it. In fact, some large RFID tagged warehouses have one of these readers installed for each section so the entire warehouse can be searched or inventoried in just a few seconds.[14] Using a similar approach, items that have been incorrectly shelved or stored can be quickly identified and put in their proper locations. This capability is especially useful for proper maintenance of library book collections and other material record facilities such as medical record archives.

These advantages compared with barcode applications allow for much faster scanning of a collection of items in a grocery cart (note that the cart does not now have to be unloaded at the checkout station), on a pallet being moved by a forklift, or shelves in a warehouse. While it will take a further decrease in passive RFID tag costs to encourage supermarkets to convert to using RFID tags, the potential advantages in reducing checkout space and checkout personnel as shown in an IBM television commercial are getting us closer to that point.[15] By adding the ability to sort out expired items in a store's inventory quickly because the RFID tag could also contain date and other desired information, additional operational cost savings are possible. This last application may even have value for consumers in the future where a refrigerator capable of reading RFID tags could alert them of out-of-date food items in their fridge, or that some items such as eggs and cold beer have run low and need restocking.

Now at this point, some of you are likely thinking "Whoa! I understand how barcode scanning can read a bunch of items at a checkout stand since each one is passed in turn across the scanner. But how can an RFID scanner read a bunch of items seemingly all at once and without having to pass each one in turn in front of the transceiver?"

This is where the added cost of an RFID tag comes in. The small microchip connected to the tiny antenna in the tag contains not only the attached item's identification information (in fact, that information could be exactly the same number as displayed on the UPC barcode label for that item) but also the ability to make some simple decisions. There are several schemes for dealing with "tag collision," the situation where a number of tags are addressed at the same time by a reader. One scheme takes advantage of the natural situation that no group consists of tags that are *exactly* alike, that is, one of them is bound to reply a tiny fraction of a second earlier than the others' response. The reader accepts that data and then sends a pulse that tells that first responder to shut down and not reply to further inquiries. This process is repeated for the remaining unread tags until all have been accounted for, a sequence of readings that typically takes less than a second to complete. Another scheme is for the reader to send out a pulse that tells all of the tags to generate a random number out of a large set of possibilities for their individual temporary ID. Given a large enough range of random numbers, it is highly unlikely there will be two random numbers in the group that will be the same. Then the reader starts down the list of possible ID numbers to read each tag in turn and tell it to shut down. The complete process is likely to finish in less than a second because each communication takes only a few microseconds.

The preceding discussion already points out that RFID technology has more data capability; it is only a matter of how complex the microchip is. For expensive items such as large flat-screen televisions, automobiles, home appliances, high-end digital cameras, and yard equipment, it could be useful to have the item's RFID tag accompany it after purchase. At point-of-sale, the store's reader could record the purchase date, store location, and even the customer's ID on the tag for ready warranty information later, should it be needed. If in-warranty repairs are required, the serviceperson could use a reader to record the call and reason for it and also program the tag with that history.

RFID applications have one disadvantage that is worth discussing. Because the tags can be read at greater distances, especially the active versions, and without the need for line-of-sight access, the ability of an unauthorized user to access their information is increased. This disadvantage has led to concerns about people reading your personal information stored on an RFID tag in your credit card or passport, a thief driving by your warehouse or a customer's residence and scanning it for desirable items to steal. While these concerns have created an aftermarket of security protection items for consumers such as metal-lined holders for passports and credit cards, there are a number of more effective methods to deal with this concern. These methods are typically designed for active RFID devices because they are more likely to be used on expensive items and to have a greater communication distance. The interchange of data can be encrypted for warehouse inventory and tracking applications and the reading distance can be reduced at the item's point-of-sale by instructing the active device on the item to switch to a low-power transmission mode.

Like other aspects of information technology, the development pace in RFID applications is also growing. For a short introduction to RFID technology and an example of the enterprise level software solutions being developed to support its use, see the online reference by Holloway.[16] For SMB supply chain managers and operations professionals, the book by Zelbst and Sower has a more recent overview of RFID technology with a number of business application examples and implementation suggestions.[17]

OCR

Optical character recognition technology has come a long way from the capability of its early days. It deserves attention here because of its value in allowing businesses to dematerialize not only some current information in paper form more easily, but also to convert some of their historical documents into a form more easily processed and shared.

Those of us who attempted to use OCR technology a couple of decades ago may recall that it often took longer to proofread the result and make the necessary corrections than it would take a trained typist to just transcribe the material directly. Processing tables of numbers was particularly time consuming, especially when the accuracy of the data was critical.

As a result, the small amount of dematerialization of paper-based information was limited to making electronic copies of important documents.

In the intervening years, many scanning solutions incorporated into commonly available office printing equipment combined with document feeders has made it easier and faster to scan large numbers of documents. Many businesses use this capability to at least reduce their older records to a form more easily stored and retrieved. However, these records cannot be edited, searched for text content, or their numerical content accessed for analysis unless the information shown in the document images is converted into digital text and numbers.

OCR capability has become faster, more intelligent, and, most important, more accurate. Enough so, that when combined with fewer transcribers that have the requisite typing speed and accuracy, it deserves another look by businesses previously discouraged from using it as a viable option for inputting data that are not in a digital form.

As an example, I printed out this sentence as you see it here with the following list of numbers, letters, and symbols—3.14159Aa Σ ® Δ λ 22C75S. The printed copy was scanned by an inexpensive (less than $149) OCR application (2010 version) for its conversion back into digital text. The scanner used was part of a common all-in-one office printer with a document feeder. The result without any editing is shown in Figure 4.4.

Note that the only problem the OCR program had was converting the Greek alphabet, a not uncommon problem when converting mathematical equations. More advanced OCR programs can be set up to handle more than one language set at a time, but the inexpensive one I used can handle only one language at a time out of a choice of number of languages. Language choice is important since part of the OCR accuracy is based on appropriate spelling to help, for example, recognize the difference between a lower-case I or a lower case L.

As an example, I printed out this paragraph as is with the following list of numbers, letters, and symbols - 3.14159Aa L ® t:,. A 22C75S.

Figure 4.4. Unedited OCR printed text conversion result. When comparing this with the original sentence, the conversion process had the most difficulty with the Greek alphabet.

A consequence of using OCR for dematerialization of information is the need for concomitant policies for secure disposal of paper documents to be discarded and for storing those documents that currently still must be retained such as deeds, original contracts, birth and death certificates, other document forms required for proof of originality. We will discuss such policies and some information disposal methods later in chapter 6. Eventually, of course, some universally recognized proof of originality for digital documents will be developed and accepted. There are some digitally signed approaches used now by some organizations, but until there is some reasonable assurance that they won't be tampered with by the many hackers out there keeping a paper document safely stored in vault somewhere significantly reduces access for such mischief.

GPS

GPS data collected in real time is usually in electronic form with location coordinates expressed in dimensions of longitude and latitude on the earth's surface. Occasionally, one will see the coordinate information for a store or restaurant printed on a business card or advertising brochure to allow a customer to enter that destination in their personal GPS navigation device. Because this entry method is awkward and prone to error, more efficient methods for users to enter these data have been developed. Most navigation devices will accept more familiar postal address information because their internal database is capable of matching that data to the more precise latitude and longitude values for that address. In other cases, the former printed location coordinates have been replaced by a QR code that can be read by the user's smartphone to input the data.

GPS systems that are more sophisticated can also determine altitude above sea level. Knowing altitude can be important in collecting business data if your product, service, or information values are affected by atmospheric pressure or the typically drier and cooler conditions at higher elevations. Accurate location data are important for transportation industries for navigation and for selecting routes that get their shipments or passengers to their destinations quickly at a minimum expense. Other useful business operations data are the current locations of capital assets, for example, trucks, forklifts, portable emergency generators, and rented equipment. An example of the use of GPS data for locating and controlling equipment and managing business operations is given below.

GPS in Farming Applications

A personal experience with how GPS capabilities have changed old familiar processes is their use on a family farm in the US Midwest. As farming equipment has become more capable and expensive many smaller farmers have taken to sharing equipment when possible. But, there is a major disadvantage in such a strategy because planting and harvesting seasons typically occur within a small time window. This limits how many farmers can effectively use a piece of equipment such as a tractor, particularly since such use is traditionally limited to daylight hours.

GPS applications have changed this situation significantly for the better in recent years. After the US Defense Department removed the resolution limitation for civilian use in 2000, the accuracy of the location data improved to less than 10 feet for many individual user applications. With advances in processing capability, higher-end GPS-based equipment can define positions with centimeter-level accuracy.

Farm equipment manufacturers took advantage of this technology by equipping their tractors with GPS guidance systems that now allow a tractor to plow a field in total darkness. This increases its available hours of use during the typical days for planting and harvesting in Illinois by nearly 90%. Although the guidance unit normally controls the tractor for cultivation processes, a human driver is still required for safety if there is an equipment malfunction or other need to take control.

When the exact location of a tractor on a field is known, a number of farm management solutions become easy to implement. One example is mapping the crop yield on a field by collecting the output yield from a harvester in real time and saving it versus the real-time position of the harvester. This can help determine which parts of a field need additional fertilizer or irrigation. Using a fertilizer applicator with an output that can be controlled in real time, the crop yield data can be used the following year to apply fertilizer more effectively.

CHAPTER 5

Alphabet Soup—Big Data, Cloud Computing, DSS, ERP, VoIP ...

The amount of information a business needs to acquire, process, transfer, store, and protect to remain competitive is increasing ever more rapidly. Eventually, the size, complexity, and rate of accumulation of data becomes too much for a business to process and manage in a timely and accurate manner using only internal resources. In 2001, Doug Laney described this situation in a Meta Group publication[1] using the terms volume, velocity, and variety to describe the increased amount of data, the reduced amount of time allowed to process it, and the increased lack of structure in that data.

Some large enterprise companies have the technical skills and capital resources to develop their own suite of software applications for managing these huge data sets associated with their operations, accounting, purchasing, planning, forecasting, customer relations, research, and other activities. An example of the typical set of applications used today by a large company is shown in Figure 5.1.

However, most organizations do not have either the skill or the resources to develop their own solutions, particularly if their core business offering is not highly technical or information intensive in nature. This is particularly true for small- to medium-sized businesses (SMBs) who might have some staff with the requisite software skills, but what staff they may have is usually needed for other business needs. Small businesses typically use spreadsheets for internal information processing combined with a choice of the many small accounting and invoicing programs commercially available for handling customer and financial information. Another significant

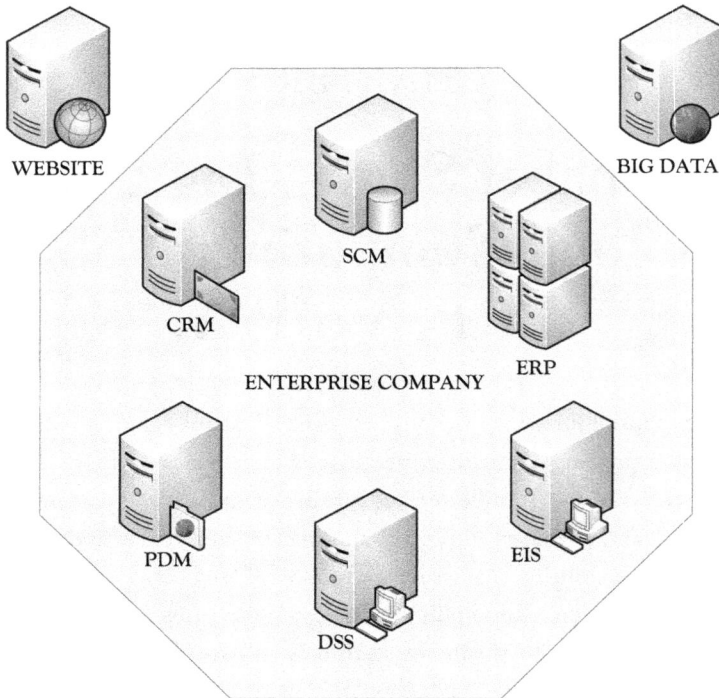

Figure 5.1. The alphabet universe of information applications used by a typical large enterprise company.

limitation for SMBs is the operating expense to support an internal hardware and network infrastructure to handle large sets of data.

As organizations grow in size, their management teams increasingly look outside for more comprehensive software solutions and infrastructure providers to manage their business processes. Transitioning part or all of their information processing needs to external suppliers is often frustrating and more difficult because many employees often prefer using Excel or other spreadsheet software solutions for their personal information processing needs. This is particularly true if the transition requires major changes in how information is entered and retrieved to adapt internal processes to those used by the selected vendors.

Selecting an enterprise software solution best suited for your business is not easy. Some of these software suites are well integrated, that is, they make the best use of information across an organization to reduce errors and costs while also improving performance. Some other suites are a collection of essentially standalone applications that usually work very well within different internal host functions, but, because they are not well integrated, sharing and comparing information among the functions can be very difficult. Other disadvantages of a nonintegrated approach are the creation of duplicate data systems, isolated functional area decisions that often conflict with decisions made elsewhere in the company, and increased operating expenses.

In addition, many businesses do not have a good understanding of what their processes do, what is required by each process, what other processes are dependent on each process, and, in some cases, are unaware that a process critical to their business even exists. The smaller the business, the more likely this is to be true. These hidden processes, I will call them "ghost" processes, often come to light when an employee retires or otherwise chooses to leave the company. Sometime in the past, it is often likely that the employee encountered a problem that occurred often enough that he or she developed a process for dealing with it, incorporated that process in their daily work, but did not document it.[2]

Even when a business has done a good job of understanding and documenting its more critical processes, problems can arise when the business grows large enough to want to take advantage of outside software solutions and information infrastructure suppliers. SMBs need to recognize that commercially available solutions[3] are based on using standard sets of common processes designed for different classes of businesses such as retail sales, manufacturing, food products, service industries, and financial firms. Often, the processes in an SMB are quite different, sometimes for good reason because of the particular uniqueness of that SMB product or service offering. But, consequently, this situation requires either a substantial revision of the SMB's processes to use an externally developed enterprise-level software solution or considerable expense and delay to have the providers of a solution adapt their software to the SMB's needs. A caveat to be considered here is that during the initial set-up and growth of a small business, its management would be wise to adapt standard processes for common activities and only develop custom processes for those parts of the business where they can provide a competitive advantage.

A combination of the situations described in the previous two paragraphs often results in one of the horror stories in the business and financial press about a company that tried to implement a new enterprise software solution and the result was disastrous for the company. Sadly, in today's news, environment disasters are usually more interesting news than successes. More companies benefit from adapting enterprise software solutions to improve their business performance than companies who do not benefit from trying to do the same. That said, there are lessons to learn from such failures and it needs to be recognized that some successful implementations were more difficult to achieve than others.

Big Data

The term "Big Data" used now even by the public news media and cited in some recent governmental programs is still relatively new to the information technology environment where its use is the most appropriate. While its origin is hazy[4] and its definition is still in the forging stage, Big Data is rapidly becoming part of the IT vocabulary in many businesses. When does the amount of information used by a business grow large enough to be called Big Data? In other words, how big is Big? The simple answer is "It depends."

In appendix A, "Big Data" is defined as "A collection of data whose very size, rate of accumulation, or increased complexity makes it difficult to analyze and comprehend in a timely and accurate manner." This means that its use depends on the viewpoint of the user of a given data set. What is huge from a small business viewpoint is likely to be a small daily consideration for a large enterprise organization. For the purpose of this monograph, a better definition would be that a Big Data situation exists when the amount of information used by a business grows large enough, is accumulating fast enough, or is increasing in complexity (becoming more unstructured) enough that the business needs to seek outside assistance and resources to use its information effectively. Hence the scope and size of the outside solution will be commensurate with the amount of information, that is, a wide variety of business intelligence (BI) solutions are available to:

- analyze enormous data sets such as search engine histories, census records, or online POS data to identify correlations, trends, and other predictive relationships;
- monitor in real-time large amounts of operational data in businesses such as oil refineries, public utilities, transportation networks, and financial systems to prevent failures or to react quickly to reduce loss of life or damage when they do occur; or
- process a wide range of unstructured information sources such as images,[5] customer information, and political conditions to support risk analysis, forecasting, and other decision processes.

We could really get mired down in the weeds here attempting to describe all of the BI solutions currently available and what are the advantages and disadvantages of each solution. But it would be a futile effort, given their equally rapid evolution to keep up with the increasing amounts of information. In fact, this book required literally continual revision during its preparation to keep up with the changes in information technology and the new management concerns those changes have created.

That said, one application reported recently in the news media illustrated how Big Data methods were used to provide information about the spread of influenza outbreaks more quickly than was previously possible using traditional medical reporting techniques. It is important to note that the individual data entries analyzed were not the result of answers to questions like "Is there a flu outbreak in your area?" or "Do any of your friends have the flu?" Instead, this was done by correlating the number of online searches conducted by individuals using flu-related terms with their location and other data such as posts and tweets about being sick, change in demand at major e-tailers for illness treatment items, and so forth.

Another example might be an analysis of the GPS-related transaction described in chapter 4 where a smartphone user submits a query on his or her phone regarding where they might buy an item they want and what the available price is at each location. Because advertisers like to focus their smartphone advertisements on people likely to respond to them, it would be useful to know the average distance a customer is likely to travel in response to the answers to their query. In addition, is there any correlation between that distance and the price of the item, that is, will the customer on average travel further for a lower price and how much? All that is needed is the customer's location when they make the request and POS data at the store where they choose to buy the requested item. Obviously, some customers value their privacy more than others and will turn off their smartphone's GPS locator and pay cash for their purchase, thus reducing the amount of data available regarding their particular transaction. But their request is still processed over the Internet using a cell phone network, providing some data regarding the rough location of the request and when it was made. By processing thousands of such transactions every day, even with parts of each transaction's data missing, Big Data analysis techniques can provide a reasonably accurate estimate of the average distances traveled and other typical values of interest regarding such transactions.

The solutions for the largest data sets depend on the use of the Internet or specialized networks for connectivity, or both, the sharing of many hardware systems for processing and storage, nonrelational database designs, and software systems designed to manage such analysis using parallel processing. Such solutions are too expensive and often unnecessary for many SMB applications. Depending on the nature of an SMB data set, the information processing solution involves choosing what the business can best do internally and what it needs to export to external providers. One approach growing in popularity is the use of cloud computing for basic data storage and information processing applications; in essence, returning to the basic concept of central mainframes accessed by user terminals used in the 1950s and 1960s. The big differences are that the mainframe is now likely to be a collection of hardware systems located in different geographic locations and the terminals are likely to have more individual computing power than mainframes of the 1980s and early 1990s.

Cloud Computing

There are a number of descriptions regarding what is cloud computing or is not, all of them lacking different aspects of the technology depending on the interests of a particular group of users. Perhaps the use of the term "cloud" came about because of this ambiguity. Cloud services use a combination of computer and network hardware installations that are usually geographically distributed in areas where the utility and other operating costs are low. These installations are connected together using the Internet and managed in a way that appears to each business user as if they were using a dedicated set of workstations and a single storage system. In reality, this management process is dynamically sharing a business's data storage and information processing across a number of available servers and network connections. This virtualization approach enables the cloud service to use each of their pieces of equipment at near its full capability, reducing the operating expenses and capital investment required to provide the desired level of service to their customers. This allows multiple instances of a word processing program to be running at the same time for different users without conflict.

If we look at the basic services provided by the more common view of the cloud computing concept, it is not unlike the use of mainframe computers in large enterprise companies back in the 1960s and 1970s as mentioned in the previous section. Users accessed these large-for-the-period computer systems via terminals to use them for information processing, retrieval, and storage. Cloud computing is essentially an updated version of that solution with a number of new features and some significant differences. Some of the advantages of cloud computing advertised by its providers are as follows:

- Cloud users can use online software applications on an as-needed basis instead of having to pay for individual workstation licenses.
- Businesses have access to the latest versions of software applications.
- Data security solutions used by cloud providers are often more robust than those used by many SMBs.
- Data can be stored online, eliminating the need for hardware to store it locally. Online data storage can eliminate the need for internal backup processes. The exception, of course, is for critical data that a business does not want to risk on the Internet.
- Online data storage is more accessible to supply chain partners, other locations of the business, and collaborators such as researchers, and outside consultants.
- Lower overall cost.
- Provides easy access by mobile device users.

- Storage capacity can be added as a business requires it.
- For memory-intensive applications such as image and video editing and large graphics creation, cloud computing software versions can be much faster.
- It reduces the number of local IT support staff required.
- It minimizes the capital investment required for IT processes.

While it can be said that all of these claims are true, what is missing is the potential effects on a company's risk management, security, and operations strategies. What are the disadvantages of cloud computing? To paraphrase an old adage, "One should be cautious about putting all of one's IT cookies in one jar!" Because the managerial questions that should be asked here are very similar to those that should be asked when considering the use of any information processing or handling solution, we will discuss those questions together with other considerations later in chapter 6.

Some cloud computing disadvantages and risks are as follows:

- The need for broadband access by a business using cloud computing for daily operations. Potential conflict can occur if business is also using VoIP systems for communications and the business's Internet connection does not have enough bandwidth or adequate data rates, or both.
- An increase in communication expenses to pay for the substantial increase in data traffic required to run the business.
- Businesses must still invest in printers, scanners, input terminals, and other I/O equipment to enter and retrieve data from the cloud.
- If a business is using some cloud-supported services to manage all or part of its daily operations the response times between the cloud and some equipment may not be fast enough for real-time control of critical activities, particularly at times when the cloud experiences higher levels of user traffic.
- If a business chooses to move its word processing, spreadsheet, and other office software applications to a cloud, there may be a limit to how many users for a client can use that cloud software at the same time. While not usually a concern for a business with only a small number of employees, this disadvantage can be a serious obstacle to

businesses if they need to expand their workforce to satisfy a rising demand for their services or products.

- Any failure or interruption of the cloud services can have a major effect on the ability of a business to continue working.
- Business data are exposed to greater security threats like denial-of-service attacks on cloud service providers.

Like all disadvantages, there are strategies to prevent some of them from occurring or to mitigate their effects when they do occur. It is important to develop such strategies *before* they are needed.

Decision Support Systems

Like cloud computing, there is no single definition that encompasses all of the manifestations of what could be called a decision support system (DSS).[6] My first boss could easily be classified as a decision support system because of all of the mentoring he provided me. For that matter, a dartboard on the wall of your office with areas labeled with various decision choices could be considered a crude decision support decision by some. However, for the purpose of this discussion, we will consider only DSS software applications.

The term "support" is important because we are talking about applications that do not make actual decisions here. The final choice is left up to the user. The application helps the user in making that choice by processing large amounts of data and providing the results in a summarized format that is easier to interpret. Recall our earlier discussion in chapter 2 about human beings being much better at comparing things than quantifying them; DSS applications often process quantitative data so that it can be presented in a format for comparison. Excel Pivot Tables are one example of this approach. An example of their use for comparing two store locations is given at the end of appendix C.

In the 1980s, a number of software applications were written for individual users and managers as the availability of personal computers in the workplace increased. Among these was a group of programs intended for use in making decisions in areas where there were no defined formulas available that a user could use to avoid their need to make a judgment call for a decision. The terminology often applied to such applications was artificial intelligence (AI) or expert systems based on the expectation that a computer could be programmed to analyze complex sets of often ambiguous data and make a decision that could be supported by users with limited knowledge about the situation. The idea was that by correlating a number of decisions made by recognized experts in a field with the sets of data they used for their decisions, one could come up with a set of rules that a program could use to analyze future sets of data and make a decision for the user entering the data.

The more popular areas of interest for these applications were employee performance evaluations, credit approval decisions, and other processes where an expert's experience and intuition was often a major part of such decisions. The problem, of course, was that the technology of the day made it very difficult to quantify such experience and intuition in any meaningful way. As a result, such applications faded in popularity and all but disappeared by the end of the decade. Today, the intuitive and experience components of decision making are usually left up to the user.

Recent advances in predictive analytics and the growth of Big Data information have created a new interest in AI and expert system applications. A number of applications are being developed for decision making in situations where the influence of personal experience or intuition is perceived to be quite small. The decision rules in such applications are constantly updated by real-time analysis of the results of previous decisions and the sets of data used to make them. That is, the application learns from its past success and failures and adjusts its decision algorithms to increase the probability of success for its next decision. One place this approach is being put to use is preventive maintenance scheduling.

There are three categories of DSS applications determined by the scope of their coverage:

- General-purpose tools intended for individual use. Many of these are available as functions or macro utilities in spreadsheet programs.[7] Other examples are the process modeling and mapping functions in some graphics software programs and a number of statistical process control (SPC) applications. Some simple "dashboard" tools such as the sparklines and conditional formatting of data discussed in chapter 2 are being used by managers to draw their attention to more significant changes in data reports. Some other examples for displaying data are presented in the book by Chaffe-Stengel and Stengel.[8]

- Applications specially designed to satisfy the decision support needs within a particular function or department in a business. In addition to the classical accounting and payroll applications, these include scheduling applications and customer relationship, product data, and vendor relationship management programs.

- Enterprise level packages used to support and coordinate decisions that affect all or at least most of a company's activities. Some examples are executive information systems and enterprise resource planning applications.

As the scope and complexity of decision support needed by a business grows, more care must be taken in choosing an appropriate DSS application. For example, an application designed for the decision support needs of a hotel business will likely be a poor choice for a manufacturing-to-stock business and vice versa. In addition, cloud computing users must consider whether or not a cloud-based DSS solution is a better choice than an internal DSS installation, especially if their other processes are using a combination of internal and cloud-based applications.

For more information about DSS concepts and its terminology, see the book by Power,[9] chapter 2 on collaboration systems in Kroenke,[10] and chapter 9 on decision making in Baltzan et al.[11]

CRM, SCM, PDM, MRP

A pantheon of standalone software applications for managing the relationships between customers, internal business functions, supply chain partners, vendors, and other business operation areas has come into existence since the use of information technology and databases became available at the individual level. These applications manage the information that needs to be shared and collect and analyze performance data with the goals of identifying potential problems quickly, improving process results, and reducing operation costs. Depending on the company's business model, some applications may become an integral part of another larger application, such as an ERP program, especially if the information both applications use and share is more effectively stored in a common database.

The following discussion describes a few of the more commonly used applications, the data of greater interest to each of them, and the business environments that are more likely to use them. It is important to recognize that whatever set of applications a given business chooses to use, the databases containing the information they need must be managed in a manner that prevents unnecessary duplication of data and inconsistent methods for entering any shared data such as customer or supplier names, invoice numbers, and filenames. We will discuss procedures and management strategies for achieving this in the data standardization segment of chapter 6.

CRM

Customer relationship management uses POS data, warranty return information, technical support records, customer satisfaction survey entries, and other customer transaction information to maintain and possibly improve the relationship between a business and its customers. Sometimes the CRM application is managed by a company's marketing function; in other businesses it may be a tool for the sales organization and expanded to cover the customer ordering processes.

SCM

A close cousin of CRM (in fact, they may be one and the same in some businesses), supply chain management applications can range in scope from just managing the interactions between a business and its suppliers to a more full-blown application managing all aspects of the supply chain, including vendor selection, supply quality monitoring, purchasing process management, shipping, warehousing, and retailing (particularly if the company is an e-tailer). Information of particular interest to SCM applications is lead-time information for purchasing, shipping times, in-process losses such as theft and handling damage, shipment errors such as incorrect quantities and wrong addresses, pipeline inventory, and economic factors.

PDM

Product data management applications are more common in manufacturing businesses because of the substantial amounts of information required by today's fabrication processes. Tracking changes in specifications, bills of materials (BOM), and machine settings is a common need along with managing process control and performance data and maintenance information.

They also can be used by businesses whose products are based on information to track document revisions, inventories of printed materials, clip-art collections, and image files.

MRP

Materials requirements planning applications were among the first information processing applications to be developed for businesses. First introduced in the early 1960s, they were used by sales and operations planning (SOP) functions to manage their production schedules and inventories of materials, purchased parts, and finished items using demand estimates and summaries of the bills of materials for each product to be produced. Today, many small manufacturers are able to duplicate the capability of earlier versions of MRP by using a combination of linked Excel spreadsheets. I developed an example of such a solution using an imaginary company making two products to create a series of assignments for operations management students. One Excel sheet contained a monthly demand forecast for the coming year, and another contained the bill of materials (BOM) for the two products with associated assembly times or purchasing lead times for each item on the list. A third sheet contained inventory information for each item, and purchasing data such as lot sizes, minimum safety stock levels, and order placement frequency for each item that need to be purchased. A fourth sheet contained the master production schedules for each product on a monthly basis and the fifth sheet showed all of the purchasing or production schedules for each item in the BOM. Students were shown how much of the schedule information on the last two sheets could be obtained automatically using appropriate formulas linked to selected parts of the information available on the first three sheets. For a more detailed example of how such information is used in a simple MRP program, see the work posted by J. E. Beaseley[12] on the Internet. The URL for his posting is listed under his name in the References.

MRP-II

As time went on and businesses became more aware of the usefulness of an MRP application, more capabilities were added to include financial information, human resource requirements, and capacity constraints. To differentiate from earlier versions, the newer versions are now called manufacturing resource planning applications (one of those all-too-often situations where the meaning of an acronym used in business depends on the context of the associated discussion.)

Enterprise Resource Planning (ERP)

Enterprise resource planning applications integrate many of the applications previously discussed with other business functions such as accounting, transportation, training, quality, maintenance, and marketing to form a single comprehensive business knowledge management solution. While many services businesses consider ERP to be useful only to a manufacturing business, many of the commercially available ERP offerings are readily adaptable for larger service providers. Some of the advantages of an ERP application are:

- Reducing the number of databases required by a business. Ideally, all of the business information is consolidated into one central database. Before the Internet this was difficult to do for large companies with more than one location, especially if those locations were in different countries.
- Gives management a cross-functional view of the business. This helps avoid overcommitting a function and helps identify functions that are not being used effectively.

- Provides a more standardized operating environment. This often helps improve in-house processes that are not performing well. It also can be a curse as we will discuss further when we list the disadvantages of ERP.
- Improves the utilization of available resources, which, in turn, creates the capacity for meeting increases in demand or a reserve, or both, for unexpected schedule disruptions. This also can free-up some skilled labor for process improvement and new product development activities.
- Can reduce overall costs caused by data errors, miscommunication between functions, and undetected disruptions in the supply chain.
- The process of implementing an ERP application often reveals business processes that are no longer needed, are outdated, or even duplicated in another part of the organization.

Okay, it looks like ERP solutions can be pretty useful for a business. If so, how is it that some businesses, even large companies that would seem to benefit the most, have not yet implemented one? The answer is complicated because there are a number of reasons, some valid, some not. Some of these reasons were briefly discussed at the beginning of this chapter, but deserve repeating and some additional clarification here as they relate to ERP. Many of the reasons also apply when considering the implementation of standalone applications such as CRM or SCM.

First, ERP solutions have a poor reputation in some circles because of a number of high-profile implementation failures reported in the business media a few years ago. For an article about some of the more spectacular ones, see Wailgum.[13] This history coupled with more recent news about other failures has caused many companies to hold any consideration of implementing ERP solutions until the track record appears to be improving. Some other reasons are as follows:

- Some businesses have the expectation that implementing an ERP system will help them organize how they do business and improve their processes. While the latter assumption is essentially true, they should not expect the ERP provider to do this improvement for them. As for the organization assistance expectation, ERP providers assume that a business has already organized most of the business's activities and has some reasonable knowledge of the processes the business uses.

- ERP solutions can be VERY expensive to implement when one includes the disruption and training costs incurred by the business during its transition to ERP. Smaller businesses may find it very difficult to borrow the money for such an expense, particularly when their forecasted revenue during the implementation is likely to drop, sometimes significantly.

- Businesses operating in very competitive environments may feel that they cannot afford to take the risk of their core business processes being suspended for the length of time required to implement ERP and train their staff how to use it.

- If a business uses a number of nonstandard processes, it takes a much longer time to change over those processes to more standard ones that the ERP solution is programmed to support.

- Similarly, if a business has a number of custom processes that give it a competitive edge, it takes a much longer time and more expense to have the ERP provider convert some of their processes to agree with the business's custom processes. This can introduce as yet unknown errors in the ERP system software caused by the conversions and insufficient times to field test them.

- There can be considerable passive resistance to changing over to an ERP system by some departments or functions in the business trying to implement it. This increases the implementation time and decreases the effectiveness of ERP when it is finally installed.[14]

Many of these difficulties can be eliminated or at least reduced if a business begins looking forward to a time when the business may need an ERP system to remain competitive. This means keeping future ERP requirements in mind when improving existing processes or establishing new ones. This also means increasing the level of understanding regarding how information is used, stored, transferred, or accessed in the business. Developing an integrated information and process management methodology for the business will help support those strategies and is in alignment with most ERP approaches.

Scheduling Applications

Scheduling back office activities, customer appointments or reservations, shipments, workforce assignments, vacations, preventative maintenance, and job shop projects are a challenge for many small businesses that cannot afford enterprise scheduling solutions such as those used by major airlines and transportation businesses. Even determining how long to make the average appointment period for a hair salon or doctor's office is complicated because of all of the variables involved—varying times required per client, some clients may arrive late, how much time to allot for tidying up between clients, and so forth. I addressed this problem in my last book,[15] using an example of a typical doctor's appointment schedule. It is reproduced here for your convenience.

Determining Standard Appointment Time[16]

A doctor and a nurse are reviewing their appointment schedule to see if they can revise the average appointment time. The goal is to reduce the number of evenings working late to take care of the last patient when some of their appointments have run over. Their data shows that the average examination time for a patient takes 15 minutes. They also need an average of two minutes to prepare the examination room for the next patient and to enter the current patient's medical records into the computer. Their current appointment time is 20 minutes which allows them to take care of 24 appointment or urgent care patients in an 8-hour day. They felt that amount of time would provide enough spare time to accommodate an occasional appointment overrun, but experience indicates that it is not enough. They have not accumulated enough data to have an accurate estimate of the variability of the examination times, but they do remember that a few examinations took as long as 30 minutes.

Let's use a normal distribution to see if we can get a rough estimate on what might be a better appointment time. We will use 15 minutes for the mean time, 30 minutes as a worst-case time, and will estimate the standard deviation σ as being 1/3rd of the difference between the maximum time and the mean time = 5 minutes. We are assuming here that a ± 3σ distribution around the average time will include almost all (99.74%) of the possible examination times. I have not included the two minutes for preparation and record-keeping since this is under the control of the doctor and nurse, does not vary much from patient to patient, and can be made up in different ways that do not affect patient times.

The current overrun margin is 20 − 15 = 5 minutes or one standard deviation. Consulting a normal distribution table, the percent of the normal distribution less than or equal to 20 minutes is 84.13%, hence there is a 15.87% chance that an examination will take longer than 20 minutes. Since there are currently 24 appointment periods per day an average of 0.1587 × 24 = 3.8 appointments will run over each day. This of course does not tell us when those overrun appointments will occur during the day. If they all occur early in the day, almost all of the patients will have to wait longer for their appointment. If they all occur late in the day, the doctor and nurse will really be working late. Thus, when the overruns occur is very important for this analysis.

If the doctor and nurse increase the appointment time to 25 minutes the probability of an overrun drops to 2.28 %, less than one appointment overrun per day. But we also have reduced the number of appointments per day from 24 to 19, a capacity loss of 20.8%! This would create a need to add facilities and doctors somewhere else to take care of the five patients we are turning away.

In the example, the fact that some of the time elements vary in value, that is, they are stochastic in nature and are characteristic of many values when dealing with customers, makes even this relatively simple determination somewhat complicated to perform. Imagine how much easier it would be if the time to take care of each client never varies, that is, it is a deterministic value and everyone always arrives on time.

For job shops making an assortment of standard products, the scheduling of which product to make next and by who is often made easier by assuming standard times for making each product. However, what do you do if two of the workers have to use the same machine at the same time?

How do you handle a priority job for a preferred customer? How do you handle custom jobs that may take more or less time to do, are your workers equally capable or do they operate at different levels of proficiency?

There are a number of ways small businesses can deal with such scheduling problems and some of them will be discussed in more detail in a following book about process modeling and improvement. In the meantime, a useful reference for those of you interested in more details about developing your own scheduling solutions is the book by Pinedo.[17] You should be warned that his book requires some knowledge of higher-level mathematics to take full advantage of what he has to say.

Communication Applications

The use of landline telephone systems for business communications is declining in favor of online communications and cell phone service. Recent surveys reported in the news media indicate that more than half of adult Americans now own a smartphone and roughly one-third of them own a tablet device. A number of factors are contributing to this change.

- Consumers are becoming more comfortable with the use of e-mail for correspondence with businesses and improved business websites make it easier for their customers to use this medium.
- Governmental agencies are expanding their use of e-commerce methods for a number of interactions that used to require a citizen to stand in line for service at different governmental offices. Renewing licenses, signing up for benefits, obtaining paid postage labels and scheduling the pickup of packages, submitting tax returns, and answering taxpayer questions are now commonly handled online.
- Technological advances enhancing the bandwidth and transmission rate of Internet connections to the level that real-time transmission (streaming) of first audio and now video is now possible for many users. This is a significant development because up to relatively recently video and audio information needed to be transferred in file form and then viewed or listened to before a person could record a reply to be sent back,[18] a considerable disadvantage and delay in a two-way conversation.

- Many business process improvements now depend on the advantages provided by a mobile communications system that not only handles voice-to-voice exchanges, but also includes access to online information and even video references.

A number of VoIP (voice over Internet protocol) communication applications are available to help SMBs replace their clunky PBX (private branch exchange) installations in areas where there is adequate broadband access to Internet. Combined with a BYOD policy to reduce a business's investment in communication devices, these solutions can save money and increase a business's capability to adapt quickly to changing communication needs. By combining them with wireless networks for a company's computer systems and peripherals, office and other process arrangements can be changed easily to accommodate new employees or reorganize groups for new projects without having to move phone lines and Ethernet cables and reprogram the PBX.

Video communication applications can help businesses with more than one location or a set of geographically dispersed supply chain partners conduct face-to-face meetings between staff at different locations without the need for the delays and costs of travel. The use of these applications for online education allows students to have conferences with their professor and work with other students on projects.

Some large global companies have their own video conferencing solutions and lease dedicated fiber-optic cables to transfer the large amount of data required by the multiple displays and audio channels used to create an environment that simulates a real meeting room for the participants. For one demonstration of what this level of technology can do see the online promotional video[19] for the Halo solution developed by Hewlett-Packard a few years ago. A quick search on the web yields a number of similar demonstrations because a number of similar solutions have been developed by major communication service providers.

Although video conferencing solutions such as Halo are currently much more expensive than a typical SMB can afford or justify needing that level of performance, the seemingly never-ending pace of technological development is likely to make that level of capability in the future as affordable for an SMB as a high-definition flat-screen computer monitor is today.

In the meantime, SMBs can take advantage of a number of less-expensive video communication solutions for one-on-one video chats, small video conferences among business colleagues at different locations, and members, and online training seminars, often referred to as webinars. Some of these applications are now used worldwide. One example familiar to the most of us is the use of Skype by the news media for interviews with correspondents in far-off places.

Before closing this discussion of video communication options for businesses, it should be noted that the interest in video communication is not new as evidenced by articles published as early as the 1950s and the development of the PicturePhone[20] by Western Electric during the 1960s and 1970s. The infrastructure needs of the PicturePhone were ahead of the technology of the time, a situation that still plagues many new product offerings today, and its size and overall awkward appearance did not attract enough customers to justify its further development.

Custom Applications

A number of unique information processing and management applications have been developed to address the needs of special situations taking advantage of the advances in information technology. One familiar situation is the monitoring, control, and decision processes used to manage a nation's power distribution grid. Other not-so-familiar situations are the management systems for two large river systems in the United States, the Colorado River Basin Project,[21] and the Office of Columbia River.[22]

The scope and complexity of these river management systems make the large ERP implementations for our major corporations look like child's play when one considers the enormous variety of customer groups interested in the management outcomes, the wide range or regulations that they must operate under, the resources they have to manage are limited and the demand for them is growing, and they have little control over their variability. Furthermore, many of the demands on the different interest groups and the various state and national regulations conflict with one another. It is the ultimate make-the-best-of-a-bad-situation management challenge.

CHAPTER 6

Managerial Considerations

This chapter covers topics where an astute managerial policy, choice, or a question at the right time can reduce risk and improve overall performance for businesses requiring both traditional processes and information systems. Some of you may have jumped ahead to this chapter because you feel that you are already familiar with what business information processes are. While that may be true for some, many will find it useful to review at least some of the topics in the preceding chapters if parts of the following discussion are unfamiliar.

Author note: Most of the suggestions and management approaches discussed in this chapter are not appropriate for a micromanagement environment. The levels of detail, ranges of technical skill, and frequent periods of continuous attention to information processes necessitate delegating the responsibility for such work as far down the command chain as possible. This is particularly true when dealing with security strategies and ensuring information accuracy. My experience in several high-tech industries is that micromanagers dealing with large amounts of information are only successful if their groups are small and the manager works longer hours than do any of their subordinates. Not a great situation to be in for the manager and not an effective situation for the company the manager works for.

In the early days of IT solutions, many businesses were vertically integrated, that is, they owned and had direct control of most aspects of their business. Most of them only operated within a national environment. As a result, the amount of data to be processed was not excessive and the need for widespread communication abilities was also small. Most SMBs did not even have any computing or information processing resources other than handheld calculators, cash registers, typewriters, and a team of file clerks, accountants, bookkeepers, and secretaries; all using pens, pencils, and paper.

Today, many standalone desktop systems are more powerful and store more information than those early mainframes. As a result, many smaller businesses have found a group of desktop systems to be more than adequate for their internal information needs. However, as their demand grows and as they begin to use outside subcontractors to perform parts of their business, rely more on outside vendors for their materials, and use the Internet for advertising and communication with customers their internal IT systems become overloaded. Larger enterprise organizations experience much of the same results for much of the same reasons, but on a much larger scale. All businesses, regardless of their size, need the ability to handle an ever-increasing amount of information to remain competitive.

The range of solutions and strategies for dealing with this problem can be grouped into three categories of choices:

- Expanding a business's internal IT capability by adding equipment and technical staff to support it.
- Using one or more of the many cloud computing service packages available. These packages can be as comprehensive as an ERP solution or as simple as one that just handles a company's database.
- Using a combination of internal IT expansion and online use of individual cloud computing applications.

Expanding internal IT capability has been the primary choice for large enterprise companies because they already have a substantial IT investment and sufficient technical staff resources. This strategy is not as attractive for smaller businesses who have limited financial resources and insufficient technical staff to execute it. In fact, many of them have agreements with an outside vendor to supply them with technical support on an as-needed basis.

Using cloud computing service packages can be a good choice for a business just starting up because their processes are still being defined and it significantly reduces the capital investment in IT equipment required. For established SMBs with established processes and some existing investment in IT hardware and technical staff, this choice requires much more consideration. Like choosing and implementing an ERP or other management software solution, cloud computing applications should match up as closely as possible with a business's current processes and hardware.

Some General Guidelines and Questions to Ask

My general guidelines are that there is no free lunch in business decisions and employees usually perform according to how they think they will be rewarded. If you do not have an understanding regarding how a supply chain partner or service provider makes a profit, you should make an effort to find out for both your benefit and theirs. The best business contracts are those where each participant feels that they receive something worthwhile from the relationship. The same rule applies to employee relationships. If you do not understand what motivates employees to do a good job other than keep collecting a paycheck, you should find out. Be clear about what you expect them to do and make sure your reward systems are consistent with those expectations.

Shouldn't this be obvious? Yes, but in my personal experience I have encountered too many managers who really do not know these simple truths or choose to ignore them. Is the above easy to do? No, but it is necessary for a business to be successful. Besides, as I often told my business students, "Managers are usually expected to solve more difficult problems and ask tougher questions. How else could one justify their higher salaries?"

In the following set of suggested questions that a manager should always be asking, a number of different topics can be used to fill in the blank underlined part of the questions. Within the context of this monograph, we should use the following topics: communications, data storage, information, data input, data retrieval, supply chain, and customer.

- What are our _____ expenses?
- How secure are our _____ processes?
- How reliable are our _____ processes?
- What parts of our _____ processes are the most critical?
- What parts of our _____ processes have the most variability?
- Which of our _____ processes needs the most improvement?
- What are the potential risks related to our _____ processes?

Preventing Problems and Improving Performance

One important part of good management is preventing problems before they occur and minimizing any consequential damage if they should occur. Some effective actions that should be done in this regard *before you need them* are:

- Establishing clear policies regarding what should and should not be done. This includes any appropriate boundary conditions or other constraints.
- Designing processes to minimize errors.
- Developing plans to respond quickly to problems.
- Training employees regularly regarding policies and execution of response plans, stressing that it is their responsibility to follow policies for the best interests of everyone.
- Reviewing policies as part of the business's planning processes to keep the policies up-to-date, discard ones no longer needed, and develop new ones needed to meet new challenges.

Another important part of good management is establishing practices and developing strategies that will reduce operating costs, increase revenue, and improve the quality and value of the product or service offered by the business. While the above management responsibilities apply to all parts of a business, we will concentrate here on those aspects associated with the use of information within a business. Areas of consideration include:

- Information handling policies
- Protection of critical business data
- Cyber security considerations
- Data standardization and customization
- Information cost factors

Information Handling Policies

Many of the issues that managers encounter are related in some form to the information required or provided by the business. Incorrect or insufficient information can lead to the wrong business decision, cause a manufacturing line to fail, expose the business to liability risks, and mislead customers. Conflicting information confuses employees and customers, diverts resources to resolve these conflicts, and delays the ability of the business to respond to a problem or make a final decision. Unauthorized access to information can compromise the company's ability to operate, provide competitors with proprietary information, and erode customer trust in the business protecting their private information. The loss of information or an interruption in the access to it can be damaging to the company depending on the extent and duration of such losses or interruptions and the importance of real-time access.

Not often mentioned is the inappropriate use of information resources during work hours, particularly the Internet, by employees. Dealing with such use will consume more and more of a manager's time in companies that do not clearly define policy regarding such use and the penalties if an employee does not follow the policy. The need for such a policy increases with the increasing use of online resources by businesses. This trend has resulted in ready Internet access at most employee workstations. An additional serious security concern is that any inappropriate use on those workstations often becomes part of a business's electronics transactions record.

An equally important area of concern that requires a clear management policy is the potential misuse of customer information by employees who have access to that database as part of their job assignment. Such misuse can be as small as getting the home phone number of an attractive fellow employee, more serious such as checking up on a spouse's daily phone calls for a friend, or clearly criminal such as stealing a customer's credit information for personal use or sale to another. It is a slippery slope to decide how serious each breach of consumer privacy is; this is an area where judgment calls should be avoided by establishing a zero-tolerance policy regarding the misuse of customer data. For example, employees are clearly told that any misuse of such data will result in employee termination and possible criminal prosecution.

More and more businesses are allowing employees to use their personal electronic devices at work, a strategy often referred to by the term BYOD, an acronym for "bring your own device." This has some advantages in that an employee whose job only requires access to the Internet now does not require the business to supply him or her a terminal or other access device and the employee can use a device he or she is already familiar with. The trade-off is an increased security risk since many employees are not as careful regarding the content on their personal phone as they should be and their phone passwords are generally easier to break if they use one at all. As the BYOD strategy becomes more widely used, it becomes all the more important for a business to establish a clear policy for employees to follow regarding the safe use of their phone *and any flash drive storage devices* at work. This policy must include clear definitions of the penalties for failing to comply with the requirements of the policy.

Protection of Critical Business Data

Every business has some data that are critical to that business's success and needs to be protected from access by unauthorized users. Such data can include proprietary operating information such as the recipe for a restaurant's signature dish, steps in an assembly process for assembling ultrasonic arrays, and manufacturing production plans. Other examples of critical information are a list of preferred customers, customer credit information, control programs for an oil refinery or electrical utility, or the design data for an upcoming new product.

In today's world of ever-increasing use of the Internet for communications and business transactions, *my first and most important advice is to keep critical information off of the Internet if at all possible. This includes not discussing the details of such information in e-mails!* Now, do not get the wrong impression here, I am not a Luddite trying to get businesses to avoid the use of the Internet. Quite to the contrary, this book's primary purpose is to inform business about the operational and competitive advantages the Internet environment can provide enterprise corporations and SMBs integrating their management of information and processes. My message is that one needs to be aware of some of the associated disadvantages, the key one being that no information can be considered to be entirely secure on the Internet.

So, what can a manager do to protect critical information and still use the Internet? More general cyber security strategies will be discussed later. For the moment, let's just discuss process changes and other policies to improve the security of critical information. First, try to limit authorized access to as few users as possible. Make a practice of encrypting such information with strong authorization passwords. Some of the information such as new product design data, proprietary recipes, and preferred customer lists can be stored separately, either internally or using a separate data storage service. Establish a strong policy of not letting employees download such information onto flash drives or personal devices neither for the purpose of taking it on a business trip nor for working at home. This is particularly important if your business has a BYOD policy that allows personal laptop or tablet computers to be used at work.

Particular care must be taken regarding the storage of individual customer credit and financial information. If at all possible, this information should be encrypted and kept separate from other POS data related to a business's customers. A number of businesses have had to notify customers in recent years that their personal identification and credit information was at risk because one of their employees lost or had their laptop or smartphone stolen with that information on it. To make it worse, in several cases the information was not encrypted and the device did not even have a password. Of course, the affected businesses said they were improving their procedures for protecting such data in the future, that response was of little solace to the customers affected by the breaches in their data security.

Critical control programs such as those controlling nuclear energy facilities, electrical transmission networks, oil refineries, and railroad traffic can be redesigned to minimize their exposure to unauthorized access or manipulated input data from external sensors and monitoring locations. As my former judo sensei said to our class, "The best defense is to not be there in the first place!" Some suggestions include hardwired control boards, boards using read-only memory for command routines, intermediate servers and Big Data analysis methods to process and verify external sensor and monitoring data, adapting control approaches currently used in commercial aviation where three redundant computers are used to process inputs for aircraft control, and dedicated communication networks isolated from the Internet for the most critical control functions. If there is a strong need to monitor the status of such facilities using the Internet, that information can be reported by the control system using a one-way communication link to an Internet monitor for further analysis.

Avoid using critical business information in cloud computing applications if at all possible. Such services have more than one business as customers and hence, a large number of individual users. This provides an equally large number of backdoor opportunities for hackers to break into some part of the cloud service's network of servers. That said, many cloud providers have more secure systems than many SMBs.

Cyber Security Considerations

This section focuses on security considerations that are more lock-and-key oriented as opposed to business security policies and process security procedures. Because it is difficult in many instances to separate these security approaches into actions that can be managed independently there will be some overlap with the discussions in other sections of this chapter. For this reason, information security is a cross-functional responsibility requiring each part of an organization to work together to ensure the safest result. To this end, there are five general security risk areas to consider:

- Management vulnerabilities
- Hardware (infrastructure) vulnerabilities
- Software and password vulnerabilities
- Employee vulnerabilities
- Disposal of data vulnerabilities
- Internet vulnerabilities

We have already mentioned the need for the parts of an organization to work together regarding cyber security. This is easier if a business develops an integrated management approach for information and other business processes, the primary focus of this book. Otherwise, potential conflicts in how security is handled in different functions can create opportunities for unauthorized users to break into your information vault. Managers concerned about cyber security need to recognize that the biggest security risk to a business is not considering first how the information necessary to the business can be intentionally or unintentionally corrupted, misused, lost, stolen, or otherwise made unusable. This means keeping managers and employees informed about potential security threats within and outside of the business.

Management

A management-related vulnerability in many smaller businesses is allowing the establishment of a number of distributed databases with different access protocols. This situation can also exist in some large enterprise organizations despite their wider use of cyber security solutions and greater knowledge of security risks. Some ways to reduce this vulnerability are discussed in the following section regarding data standardization and customization.

My years of experience of being both a contributor and a manager of groups working on information technologies and software development has made it clear that for every clever person who develops a better way to protect and secure digital data, there is at least one equally clever person who is working on a method for circumventing that protection. How many people and technical resources are working on cracking a given digital data safe and how long it takes before one of them succeeds is only a function of the level of desire for the information inside. It should be pointed out that this observation applies to nearly every security protection situation—state secrets, government witness protection, bank deposit boxes, and so forth. All one has to do to find some real-life examples is to listen to a few evening newscasts every week.

Hardware

Most hardware security solutions rely on using some software component to operate a hardware access device—fingerprint readers, retinal scanners, program keys, and so forth. The ultimate hardware security solution is to isolate the information system completely within an environment that requires physical entry to use the system.[1] Such solutions are generally impractical in today's Internet-connected world with a few notable exceptions discussed previously in the critical business data section of this chapter.

Internet access introduces a new hardware security risk, the network connections. Both hard-wired and wireless connections can be tapped in much the same way as old telephones in the J. Edgar Hoover days of the FBI. Digital data streams make it more difficult to listen in their content, much more so if the information is encrypted. But this data transmission environment is changing rapidly. For example, the same advances in technology that now makes real-time video conversations and streaming movie content applications possible also makes it easier to listen in on unencrypted data and to break the code of encrypted data faster. A number of small businesses using wireless networks to connect their internal systems to printers, data servers, and Internet modems have failed to activate the password protection for such networks or are still using the default password for network. This situation is even more common in residential areas. Some residential wireless network users do not use any passwords and are ignorant of how far the range of their wireless modems and routers can be.[2]

One area that deserves some consideration is disposing of hardware that has grown obsolete or that is no longer needed. We will talk about the aspects of what a business should do regarding such disposition of their equipment later in this section. However, what sometimes falls between the cracks is the return of rented equipment, particularly large publically shared printers and copiers. The hard drives and other memory devices used in network printers and copiers to allow them to spool the jobs can retain copies of the most recent information submitted to them. More modern versions are careful to erase those copies periodically, but some older equipment may not and their data can be retrieved later by the rental company or the next user. Hence, it is best that a policy is established regarding rental equipment return to ensure that critical data is erased securely before the equipment leaves your business.

Software and Passwords

Software access security solutions typically involve some form of password. The major problem with passwords is that the harder they are to break, the less convenient they are for the authorized user. Most users prefer a password easy to remember and type in correctly, for example, their daughter's name and birth date. That choice makes it much easier for an unauthorized user to determine what their password is, particularly in this age of Big Data when our personal information is available in scattered form all over the Internet—a reference to their favorite daughter on their Facebook page, a tweet wishing her Happy Birthday on Twitter, a full spelling of her name entered in a genealogy search engine, and so forth. Big Data analytic methods are useful to hackers too!

Okay, so you strongly encourage your employees to create stronger passwords. Keep in mind that when the passwords are long and contain hard-to-remember character sequences a new security risk will often occur. Employees will be tempted to store a reminder on a card or Post-it® note somewhere convenient in their workplace, making it easier for a visitor or passerby to obtain one or more passwords with the associated employee name since many workplace areas have nametags for their respective users. One way to help employees remember a long password without making a note of it is select a mnemonic such as the title of this book and numbers indicating which letters are used from each word, for example, 6r3n2fsdn. Also avoid a practice by some businesses to assign passwords created by using random character generators or distribute new password sets using e-mails or other electronic means. If your company policy is to change passwords periodically, require each employee to change their individual password themselves and provide them with one of the many password strength analyzers[3] to check the strength of their choice.

When there is a need for a frequent confidential conversation or exchange of information between an individual user and an institution, an exchange of passwords before full access is granted provides another level of security. An example is a client checking on the status of his or her bank account. The client enters the account ID and personal password. Once the password and account number have been verified, the bank replies with an image or other descriptor that the client chose when setting up the account. This tells the client that they are connected to the correct website. The client then enters a second password to gain full access. The security level can be enhanced further by the bank randomly picking one of several questions for the client to answer and comparing that answer to the answers supplied by the client for each question when they set up the account.

This process is important for a business serving customers. It ensures the security of their interaction with customers and also prevents a customer from being connected to another site because of an URL entry error or jeopardizing their account security by replying to a fake site in an e-mail message that pretends to be from their bank. The fake site may obtain their first password but when unable to reply with the second password entry page alerts the client to not go further and to change their entry password the next time they use the real bank site.

Employee

Often the greatest security risk is an employee who is unaware of how their daily actions can affect the safety of the company's data. Some common examples are:

- Not taking the same security precautions on their personal equipment at work as they do using the company's equipment.
- Being lax about updating passwords regularly and using an easy-to-crack password when they do.
- Connecting to insecure sites on the Internet using company assets.
- Loading music and apps from personal flash drives for use on company systems.
- Giving out passwords and other security information in response to e-mail and telephone queries from unverified users, a process used by potential intruders called "phishing."
- Interacting with their personal social media accounts during working hours or using company equipment to do it, or both.
- Not being careful about discarding information.
- Printing or copying data, particularly the more critical data discussed in the previous section, on publically shared printers and copiers.

While it is unrealistic to think you can take steps to eliminate all of these employee threats, particularly since new possibilities are being discovered every day, establishing clear policies to prevent security breaches and corruption of information and regularly reviewing them with employees is a good place to start.

Disposal

Most businesses have developed a good policy for securely disposing of paper documentation when it is no longer needed, this is particularly important when scanning in documents for dematerialization. Some documents such as contracts and deeds will need to be retained in paper form for a long time; some other original documents may still need to be kept for a specified time to comply with regulation retention requirements. A policy is also needed for disposing of electronic documents and other data. There are more things to consider since a digital file can exist in a number of places—workstation drives, different internal servers, on a cloud computing service, various cassettes and floppy disks (yes, there are still some around), CDs, DVDs, laptops, smartphones, tablets, cameras, various forms of flash drives, and the Internet.

There are two major disposal considerations: What to do with the hardware memory device, and how to more securely erase a given file? The hardware part of a data disposal policy is easier to define. The safest strategy is to physically destroy the storage medium, particularly magnetic media such as hard drives, floppy disks, tapes, and data cassettes. Just drilling holes in these devices is not enough to destroy all of the data since there will be enough of the recorded surface left to recover the information not drilled away. I have seen the data on some seriously damaged hard drives recovered even after flooding and some heat damage. Such drives are remarkably robust. If the covers are removed so that each individual magnetic surface can be accessed separately for demagnetization, that process should be adequate. Trying to demagnetize an assembled stack of magnetic disks will not reach all of the areas on the disk surfaces unless the magnetic fields involved are very powerful. Plastic media such as CDs, DVDs, and Blu-Ray Disks should preferably be incinerated after shredding just like paper documents. The advice here is to use a trusted destruction service.

The alternate strategy is to completely erase the data on the storage medium so that it can be safely used by someone else. Flash memory can usually be safely reused by reformatting the memory two or so times. Plastic media devices like CDs and DVDs are generally not amenable to secure erasure processes and are better destroyed. Magnetic media are a different situation. First, when you erase a file on a magnetic media, the file information is not erased. Only the reference to where it is stored on the media is erased and the associated data area is made available for future storage use. Until that area is overwritten several times by other data that original is still retrievable by an expert who can access all of the information on a disk without having to have a directory to find it.[4]

Because the magnetic material can retain a vestigial image of the data previously stored in a location, that image, although it gets fainter, can remain for a number of following write cycles and can be retrieved by a recovery expert. Therefore, to securely erase data, a business needs a software program that will erase the data directly, not just its reference in the disk's file directory, and do that erasure several times using random data sequences each time. Given the time and effort it takes to do this process for the large-capacity drives of today, it would be less expensive to just destroy the existing drive and install a new drive for the next computer user.

Erasing a single file or a small group of files is easier, particularly if these files are stored locally with a business. Using the multiple overwrite erasure available as part of a number of security software packages accomplishes the job provided that the disposal check lists account for all of the instances where the files are stored. This includes employee personal devices and flashdrives and the routine backups containing those files.

Erasing files on the Internet completely and securely is generally an exercise in futility, particularly if any of those files has even a remote possibility of having been accessed via CRM, e-retail transactions, attached to e-mail messages, social media postings, or search engines. Social media sites often let users easily delete information from their postings, but the data are usually still there somewhere in the database that the social network service uses to sell data to its customers. Cloud computing use is somewhat easier to ensure total erasure as long as one considers that it is unlikely erasing a file in a cloud storage server will also include its erasure in older backups by the cloud service provider. How files are erased is a question a business needs to ask of a potential cloud service solution. *Storing a file on any Internet site is as close to guaranteeing immortality for that information as one can get.*

Internet

Ah! Where to start? Like all big cities where there are parts of town where it is more dangerous to be, the Internet has its dark side too. Among all of the wonders, useful things, and other advantages for businesses, there is an army of con artists, vandals, thieves, and organizations wanting to use those advantages too. Like a visitor to a big city, a business must develop a level of caution, or "online smarts" if you prefer, to use the Internet safely. Many of the same common sense rules apply.

If an online service or product offering appears to be too good to be true, it probably isn't and at least deserves more checking and validation before accepting any of its claims. Another rule and a favorite of mine is

"There is no free lunch!" Users are offered all sorts of free services, news, entertainment, videos, investment advice, sports updates, and subscriptions; all they have to do is sign up, agree to a few rules, approve the usage license agreement, and they are good to go!

At this point, some of you are probably asking what has this to do with business. The answer is "plenty!" Some of those users are likely to be your employees. If your business uses the Internet for business activities, the realistic view is that at some time during a work day one or more of your employees will take a couple of minutes out to check their Facebook page, send a Happy Birthday! e-mail to a friend or relative, order an item, and so forth. In short, they may use one of those free sign-up services above. All of the security risks that a user would encounter accessing those services from their home computer also exist at work. Furthermore, many businesses are taking advantage of many of those same services for business reasons.

Search engines, social networks, instructional videos, free webinars provided by vendors (free training, just sign up and tell something about your business and interest in our product), and ordering office supplies are just a few of the many examples.

To be fair, most of the "free" services offered businesses do not have any evil intent. Most of them are either collecting data for their own use to improve their products, understand needs of their marketplace better, identify trends or changes in demand, or to assemble data sets to sell to others for their own. The problem is that some collection methods are more intrusive than others and hence pose greater security risks. Users have no way to know the extent of information being collected unless they read the licensing agreements for the services very carefully and carefully fill out their preferences during installation. Be honest, how many of you have actually done that?

The use of social networks for business reasons has several advantages, but also the same information collection risks discussed in the previous paragraph. The advantages are often significant depending on the type of business you are in and the customer audience you sell to. Having a Twitter account, for example, can provide immediate feedback from the customers of a services business about what it is doing well and what needs improving, avoiding the delays and expenses of external customer surveys. Having a Facebook account allows a business to communicate information about new products, changes to current products, and FAQ answers to its customers with opportunities to receive feedback about that communication quickly. Of course, what your company posts and what customers say on those social networks can easily become available to your competitors. Keep in mind that all of the social networks make their money accumulating and selling data to others. A related caution is that any information entered on the Internet never really goes away, even when you think you have taken every step to delete it. There is always a previous backup of your data somewhere.

While the author is not a big fan of social networking sites because of the limited control over what information is collected and distributed by these sites, they do have a place in today's global environment and deserve consideration as part of a business's information processes. At the least, it is recommended that a business set up accounts in its official name on these sites to prevent other users from using their name for a fake site in an effort to collect information or to post misleading or disparaging information. If the business does not want to commit a person to update those accounts regularly, they can post enough information on their front pages to direct customers to more secure sites for the information or technical support they want.

Finally, let's discuss those "free" sites and tempting online ads that intend your business harm or want to steal your information. First defense is to not click on any site or ad from any company, organization, or individual you do not recognize. There are several software security suites for businesses that can verify whether or not a website appears to be legitimate. Install these features in your business's e-mail and browser applications and also use them to screen search engine results before selecting any of the search answers for further information. Remember the rule "That if it appears to be too good to be true, it probably isn't" when you are tempted by an ad with an attractive business claim like "cut your costs in half in just 30 days!" Evil doers use such ads as an electronic Trojan horse to get by your security software in an attempt to slip some malware that will either damage your software or lie quietly in wait to collect passwords or perform other mischief. There is an ongoing battle between the software security companies and the malware designers where the security software defenses are slightly behind the creativity of the malware designer.

Data Standardization, Errors, and Customization

The importance of standardizing data collection and storage processes as much as possible cannot be overemphasized. In any business, there will be some necessary exceptions to this strategy, but they need to be managed as carefully. We are not talking about just individual process management here but the overall information strategy for the business. Interwoven with this strategy is the major influence it can have on reducing information processing costs.

A key component of many information management applications is a central database, which is one virtual or physical location for storing the daily operational and financial data for the business. In reality, it is likely to be physically distributed over a number of hardware systems, particularly if it is handled by a cloud computing solution. Therefore, the definition of central here implies that the data storage capacity is managed by a single system.

One of the advantages of this strategy is that information errors caused by duplicate entries of the same information in different formats are eliminated. For example, Ken Shaw in one database, Kenneth Shaw in another, and Shaw, K. in a third, but all referring to the same person, are now replaced by one entry, Kenneth Shaw. Now this problem could be solved by developing some pretty strict rules regarding how a customer's name is entered in different company databases, but that approach ignores the fact that a given name still needs to be entered several times (costs money to do), and the probability of an entry error still exists in proportion to the number of entry points (although lower because of the rules). It also ignores the added cost of performing multiple data entries and maintaining three separate databases.

One centrally managed database also avoids the errors caused by different database formats, that is, the shipping database lists customer address information first and the financial database lists the customer's credit information first. In this case, we could use computing power to collect and correlate information from different places, but that takes a person with the database skills to program the computer and knowledge of all of the differences in the databases to obtain an accurate and useful result (this also costs money to do). Backups of a business's data are inherently easier to do when the data storage is managed centrally. Backup storage and handling costs are also reduced.

An exception to the centralized database strategy may be required for custom data only required by one function in a business or for business critical data that a business may not feel comfortable storing in a cloud-based storage system. In such cases, it is unlikely that these sets of data will have much in common with the other information used by the business. As such, they can be managed in a separate database close to their point-of-use and with enhanced security if required. In cases where there is substantial overlap with information stored in the centralized database, the costs of maintaining and securing a duplicate data set need to be compared with the costs of expanding the centralized database and possibly increasing the security risk because of its broader exposure to unauthorized access.

Governmental agencies are often notorious for the lack of standardization in databases that later depend on each other. To be fair, when these individual databases were first set up each agency generally expected to operate on their own. Hence, there was little incentive to work with other agencies regarding some ground rules for data that might need to be shared. Many of those databases were set up using paper documents and physical filing systems. Some agencies began converting these paper systems to digital form over the past two decades but in general still kept to their original database structure. Today, these different paper-based and digital databases are one of the major causes of governmental inefficiency. While most agencies now recognize this problem, it is difficult for them to find the funding to correct the situation.

For example, many different land descriptions are used to describe the same physical location on our globe by planning commissions, county recorders, county tax assessors, title companies, mortgage companies, utility companies, county road departments, and environmental agencies. Correlating the property owners and tax assessment changes to a new wetlands proposal is frequently an exercise in frustration and often dependent on someone's personal knowledge of the area involved to clean up the confusion. Even the geographical description can be confusing when some surveyors refer to locations by referencing the owners of the adjacent properties at the time of the survey. In the future, when a legal description of the property is needed for a mortgage application, it is likely that the ownership of one or more of the referenced properties will have changed and the surveying description will be unclear. To get an updated description, the mortgage applicant has to search back through records maintained by another department using different physical descriptors.[5] Of course, the description could have been less sensitive to ownership changes by requiring that the physical description be based only on geographical coordinates, directions, distances and USGS benchmarks.

Information Cost Factors

Most managers, especially those managers in IT functions, are aware of the information processing costs associated with purchasing, operating, and maintaining computer systems, storage devices, input/output devices, network configurations, and backup systems for internal business use. Given that knowledge they are able to compare those costs on a one-to-one basis with the costs for outside services performing the same function. The danger here is using just that knowledge to determine whether or not a business would possibly benefit from outsourcing its information processes and data storage.

The problem is that there are a number of hidden information processing costs that are not included in these considerations and that can be significantly altered for better or worse by a decision to change. This is more likely to occur in companies that manage their information processes separately from their other business processes. A poor choice here could turn out to be another example of a common experience in many companies where the improvement executed by one function ends up degrading overall business performance. So, what are the costs to look for? Here are some areas to check out, not only in IT, but also in other processes in the company, even those that do not appear at first glance to have any information processing content.

- Information input processes.
  - How many data entry stations are needed?
  - How many stations would a cloud solution provide?
  - How many paper entry processes are there?
  - Could they be dematerialized?
  - If so, how many more data entry stations would be needed?
  - Could we get customers to do more of the entries?
  - If so, what equipment would be required?
- Information output processes
  - How many data output stations are needed?
  - How many printing processes are there?
  - Could they be dematerialized?
  - If so, what would be needed?
  - Could we get customers to do more of the printing?
  - If so, what process changes would be required?
- What are our backup costs?
- How many databases do we have?
  - Are they on separate servers?
  - How much of the information is duplicated? How many times or how many locations?
- What is our input information error rate?
  - What does it cost us to correct such errors?
  - What are the rate and costs for a cloud solution?
- What is our output information error rate?
  - What does it cost us to correct such errors?
  - What are the rate and costs for a cloud solution?
- What new information is needed by our business?
  - How do we collect it?
  - Where will we store it?
  - Who will use it?
  - What will it cost?
- What is our system uptime?
  - What does it cost us when it is down?
  - What is the cloud solution uptime?

- What are our office software costs?
  - How many users are there?
  - How many applications are required?
- What are the cloud office software costs?
  - How many users will it support at the same time?
  - Does it provide the same features?
  - What are the effects on our database, if any?

To be fair, smaller businesses are likely to not have some of the answers to the above questions. Often, it is because they do not yet have the resources to provide the answers, sometimes they have already chosen an outside support solution, and frequently it is because they are not sure how to measure or calculate the values asked for. If so, it is a good idea to begin acquiring such data. This will enable a business to be better prepared when it needs to consider changes or improvements in its information processing methods and resources.

For some ideas on how to measure some of these costs and associated performance measures, the book by Hubbard[6] may provide some ideas to those interested as to how to start.

APPENDIX A

Glossary

Accuracy. How closely a measurement or assessment reflects the true value. Not to be confused with precision; see **Granularity**, **Resolution**, and **Precision**.

Attribute. In the context of information, a descriptor that is not usually associated with a numerical value. Some examples are bad, excellent, red, green, tall, small, wide, far, heavy, fast, portrait, and scenic.

Back Office. A term used to denote those activities in a service process that can be performed without interaction with the customer.

Barcode. A pattern of alternating black and white lines, often of varying widths, for labeling products and other items.

Big Data. A collection of data whose very size, rate of accumulation, or increased complexity makes it difficult to analyze and comprehend in a timely and accurate manner.

Blog. An online collection of information or discussion posted by an individual or group of individuals.[1] While the range of topics can be very broad, it is typically limited to a selected area of interest. The term reportedly is a contraction of two words (web log).

Brick and Mortar (B&M). A term used to describe a physical business location.

Business Intelligence (BI). A term often used to describe the range of analysis approaches used to process business data. Some examples are data mining, forecasting, trend identification, and linear programming.

Cloud Computing. A business strategy where part or all of an organization's information processing and storage is done by online service providers.

Customer Relationship Management (CRM). The management of current and future customer interactions with a business. This can include sales support, warranty and technical support activity, Internet website, marketing, and product advertising.

Cross-Functional Diagram.[2] A process diagram where each activity is depicted in a column or row corresponding to the functional area that performs the activity.

Cross-Functional Software. In the context of this book, software applications that share data across different functions in a company and process that data to achieve the purpose or mission of the business. Examples of this type of software are ERP, MRP, CRM, VRM, and PDM applications.

Cyclic Redundancy Check. A process for verifying that a data packet was transferred without any errors. More sophisticated versions of this process also provide enough information to correct detected transmission errors.

Decision Support System (DSS). Information processing application used by managers and business professionals to analyze situations, monitor and compare performance data, highlight changes that require their attention, and to identify the more promising solutions. DSSs are one component of the overall MIS content for a business.

Delivery Point Bar Code (DPBC). Version 4 of the POSTNET barcode format used by the US Postal Service.

Dematerialization. Changing from a tangible to an intangible form. For example, scanning a photographic negative or paper document to a digital file.

Deterministic. Having a predictable value with a very narrow range of variance. As a result, deterministic values do not require the use of probability distributions to describe their behavior in business analysis methods or decisions and can usually be represented by a constant value. See **Stochastic**.

e-commerce. A term used to describe interactions between businesses and customers using the Internet.

Enterprise Resource Planning (ERP). Expansion of MRP activities to include the coordination of other supply chain activities such as shipping, ordering, warehousing, and quality assurance. See **Manufacturing Resource Planning**.

e-tail. Retail business conducted online using the Internet (B2C interaction).

Flash drive: In the context of this monograph, a semiconductor memory device, typically the size of a pack of chewing gum, and usually accessed using a USB port.

Flowcharting. A graphical method for depicting the movement of items, customers, or information though a system. Although many of the symbols were originally developed with information processing in mind, they have been adapted in various forms to map other process flows.

Format. In the context of information, a description of the way information is presented such as a graph, chart, image, table of values, sequence of numbers, sound, color, etc. See **Medium**.

Front Office. A term used to denote those activities in a service process where some participation of the customer is necessary for their completion.[3]

Geographical Information System (GIS). An information system whose base reference is a geographical or other physical location. Frequently used for business decision processes regarding location choices and logistics planning. Other major applications are mapping and navigational processes.

"Ghost" process. A term used by the author to denote a process that is often developed by an individual or a small group to deal with a problem that they need to deal with on a frequent basis. Such a process is usually not documented and not known to others, but has become essential to the business.

Hadoop. An open-source software platform developed by Apache Software Foundation for data-intensive applications where the data are often widely distributed across different hardware systems and geographical locations.

Hacking. Unauthorized access to information.

Hashtag (#). A metadata symbol used to denote the subject or topic of a discussion thread in social online media. Examples as might be related to this book are #bigdata, #internethistory, and #overbooking.

Granularity. A term sometimes used to describe the level of detail used in obtaining information. In chemically based photography, it could be used to describe the density of silver grains in a photographic film or paper. Also see **Resolution** and **Precision**.

Information. In the context of this book, a collection of descriptors derived from observation, measurement, calculation, inference, or imagination in a form that can be shared with or communicated to others, or both. The format can be tangible or intangible or some combination of both.

Intelligent Mail Barcode. The most recent bar code used by the US Postal Service, sometimes referred to as the OneCode Solution.

International Standard Book Number (ISBN). A number assigned to a book to allow it to be uniquely identified. Both the number and a barcode of the number are typically displayed on a book's cover.

Internet of Things (IoT). A term used to describe the community or collection of people and items that use the Internet to communicate with other.

Keyword. An identifier attached to unstructured data to allow that data to be searched in a structured manner. Common keywords for images are location (sometimes automatically added by a GPS chip in the camera), time, day, year, event name, person's name, and so forth.

Little's Law.[4] An observation that the ratio between given average line length and waiting time values is characterized by the average arrival rate value for all waiting line models. That is, the average arrival rate is equal to the average waiting line length divided by the time spent waiting in line ($\lambda = L/W$).

Makespan. The total time required completing a group of jobs in manufacturing. For waiting lines, this corresponds to the total amount of time required to process a group of waiting customers.

MapReduce. An early Big Data (before this term became popular) programming solution originally developed by Google for parallel processing using very large data sets distributed across a number of computing and storage systems. A Hadoop implementation of MapReduce is now available.

Management Information Systems (MIS). The full range of information technology solutions required by a business to run its daily operations, support strategic planning and process improvement activities, and identify issues requiring management attention for their resolution. See **Decision Support System** for an example of one of the components of MIS.

Manufacturing Resource Planning (MRP-II). The coordinated management of purchasing, inventory, bills of materials, financial data, human resource needs, and production scheduling processes to meet a forecasted demand.

Materials Requirements Planning (MRP). The coordinated management of purchasing, inventory, bills of materials, and production scheduling processes to meet a forecasted demand. Predecessor of MRP-II.

Media. The variety of information communication processes.

Medium. In the context of information, the method used to transfer information from one point or person to another point or person. Examples are paper, film, tape, audio, television, radio, photographs, displays, satellite transmission, code, and digital files.

Memoryless. A condition where a value is independent of any previous value. That is, it can be said that the value has no memory of any preceding values. This is an important characteristic when dealing with probabilistic values. For example, the result of a coin toss is not affected by the result of the previous coin toss.

Metadata. This term can mean a number of things depending on the context in which it is used. It can denote how a set of information is structured, such as the ISBN values assigned to books, the format of the UPC barcodes, and the Library of Congress classifications used in catalog books. It can also be a keyword assigned to a set of data to make it more easily searched for. For example, the list of keywords at the beginning of this book or the definition for hashtag used in online text message exchanges.

Management Information Systems (MIS). The software applications and computer hardware systems in an enterprise that provide information for management decisions regarding its business operations. Also see **Decision Support System.**

Newspaper Model. A strategy for determining the optimum order size to best satisfy the forecasted demand of newspapers or other types of products whose value diminish significantly after some date.

Noise. In the context of this monograph, anything that interferes with the successful processing and communication of information or affects its accuracy.

Optical Character Recognition (OCR). Technology where a scanned digital image of a printed page is analyzed to convert the text into an editable and searchable format.

Overbooking. A yield management strategy where more reservations than the number of opportunities available are accepted based on the assumption that some reservations will be cancelled or not show up when the time for providing the reserved service occurs.

Parity Bit. Additional data appended to the end of a data packet by the transmitting system that can be used by the receiving system to detect the occurrence of an error during transmission. See **Cyclic redundancy check.**

Phase. A single step for a service or manufacturing process.

Point of sale (POS). Useful information regarding what is purchased, the nature of services performed, and the types of customers served can be gained by a business analyzing the data collected from its sales transaction processes. These include the customer ordering, shipping, and payment processes.

POSTNET. Postal numeric encoding technique. A barcode standard used by the US Postal Service to display Zip code information more clearly on envelopes and packages for automated sorting equipment.

Precision. The level of detail included in information, such as the number of decimal places in a number, the number of pixels/inch in an image (resolution), or other measure reflecting how closely information is observed. Not to be confused with **Accuracy** defined elsewhere in this glossary.

Process. In the context of this book, a necessary sequence of steps required to provide a desired result. That result can be tangible or intangible or a combination of both.

Product Data Management (PDM). Management of all information related to a product during its life cycle. This includes the specifications, user documentation, bill of materials, reliability data, warranty failure reports, engineering changes, and all design files.

QR code. A two-dimensional graphic code format used for quick input of more information than UPC barcodes can provide. When scanned by the camera in a smartphone, it can be used to link the user to an Internet site displaying the additional information.

Relational database. A database for storing structured data. This allows for a fixed format, usually a limited number of values in a defined order.

Resolution. A term normally used to describe level of detail in an image (pixels/inch, total pixels/image), or how precise a value is.

Risk. In the context of business decisions, the cost of a particular outcome. When a set of outcomes are possible, this cost is often weighted by the probability, if known, of that particular outcome occurring. Not to be confused with uncertainty, a term often used incorrectly to communicate the level of risk.

Service Blueprint. A process diagram for services where the activities are separated into two groups: customer involvement required (front office) and support behind the scenes (back office). Sometimes the service blueprint adds a third group of activities where customer involvement may or may not be required depending on the particular circumstances (like when a credit card is rejected or approval for repairs after the diagnosis is completed).

Service Distribution. The variability in the service time. This variability can be represented by selected probability distributions to best fit the particular situation, with the exponential distribution being most commonly used.

Service Rate. The average number of items serviced or processed per some selected period of time. This continuous value can have a decimal component for small service rates, but is normally rounded to whole numbers for larger rates. Some typical values are: 5 megabytes per second, 1.2 customers per minute, 6 cars per hour, or 120 products per week.

Service Time. The time required to perform a service or process. The average value is the inverse of the average service rate.

Show rooming. A term used to describe the actions of a potential customer checking out a product in a store to see if it is what they want and then buying that product elsewhere, usually online, where they can get a lower price.

Statistical Process Control (SPC). A methodology used to ensure product or service quality at a minimum expense. Although commonly thought to be a manufacturing quality strategy, SPC principles also can be applied effectively to ensure the quality of information or service process results.

Stochastic. Having an unpredictable value because of the possibility of a wide range of possible results. As a result, stochastic variables must be represented by either discrete or continuous probability distributions in analysis or decision methods such as overbooking, forecasting, waiting line, or risk assessment applications. Also see **Deterministic.**

Stock Keeping Unit (SKU). How a product is tracked in inventory. The product can be an individual part, a subassembly of individual parts, or a quantity of individual parts (e.g., a single bottle, a package of six bottles, or a case of 24 bottles, each with its own SKU number).

Swim-Lane Diagram. Another name for a cross-functional diagram.

Tag. There are two definitions in this monograph, depending on the immediate subject matter. 1. A qualifier attached to unstructured data, usually an image, to enable it to be searched for, grouped into categories, or sorted. See **Keyword**. 2. A device or label attached to physical items to allow their easy identification and tracking.

Tag Collision. A situation that occurs when an RFID tag reader attempts to read a group of tags all at once. A number of interrogation schemes have been developed to handle this situation.

Tweet. A brief text message of no more than 140 characters posted on the Twitter social networking site.

Uncertainty. A situation where the set of possible outcomes is stochastic in nature. Not to be confused with the concept of **Risk** defined elsewhere in this glossary.

Uniform Code Council (UCC). Organization responsible for administering the Universal Product Code for grocery items and other retail products.

Universal Product Code (UPC). A 12-digit barcode used by food chains and other retailers for sales checkout processes and tracking items in their inventory.

Vendor Relationship Management (VRM). Similar in concept to customer relationship management, but focused on interactions with current and future vendors (suppliers) for a company. This can include sharing of operational data, forecasts, quality assurance, failure data, and vendor certification.

Virtualization. A method for managing hardware assets used at the same time by different users or processes, or both, that makes the part assigned to each user or process appear to act as if it was running on a separate piece of equipment.

Visual Basic for Applications (VBA). A programming language used by more advanced users to develop special functions and other macro routines to enhance their program applications.

Waiting time. The time spent waiting to be processed. The average waiting time is characterized by two values: the average time spent awaiting service and the total time spent in the system (waiting plus service time).

W is often called throughput time in manufacturing applications and sojourn time in service applications.

Work-In-Process (WIP). The number of items in a manufacturing system waiting for processing or being worked on. It can also refer to the number of people in a queue waiting for service or in the process of being served.

APPENDIX B

Acronym and Symbol Definitions

Business and technology professionals are notorious for using a wide variety of three-letter and four-letter acronyms and symbols in their discussions, presentations, and literature. These often cryptic abbreviations represent the long string of words and modifiers that define some business or information technology concept or operation. Acronyms and symbols reduce the amount of typing necessary in memos and reports and, sadly, also allow much more information to be displayed on a PowerPoint slide ;-). As the emoticon at the end of the previous sentence indicates, even this author is sometimes tempted to use them. The creators of these acronyms and symbols usually do the courtesy of defining them when they are first used in a written communication or slide presentation. However, once an acronym or symbol becomes commonly used within a particular field, this courtesy definition is dropped under the assumption that everyone knows what it means. Examples of this are DVD, VCR, TV, and so forth.

Fortunately, most of these acronyms and symbols have a unique definition. But readers need to be aware that an acronym or symbol can have more than one meaning based on where it is used. For example, CD can mean one thing to a music listener (compact disk), another thing to a finance professional (certificate of deposit), another thing to a governmental worker (civil defense), and with a small change to Cd, signifies the element cadmium to a chemist. Okay, most of you will say that this is obvious. But it may not be to others in a group reviewing a presentation. Imagine a meeting for the first time between a marketing department and finance planners where the marketing team is describing the potential market size for a new CD product they want to introduce. How far do you think the presentation will go before someone asks what CD stands for? My experience is that it will go further than one would think because the average person does not want to be seen as not knowing what a term means if it is not defined at the start.

In other instances, there are different acronyms for essentially the same concept or meaning. For example, first-in-first-out (FIFO) in manufacturing and first-come-first-serve (FCFS) in service processes both convey the same priority rule. The proper usage here is being aware of the context in which the priority rule is applied.

Texting on cell phones, brief e-mails, and limited messages in social media applications have led to the creation of images (emoticons such as the one I used earlier) and a wide variety of acronyms for common phrases and expressions. To keep the list of acronyms and symbols in this appendix manageable, the entries are restricted to those more appropriate for our discussion of integrating the management of information and business processes. By choice, the symbols for various currencies are also not included.

Only basic definitions are given in this appendix. See appendix A for more in-depth definitions of more important usages.

aaS. Available as a service. This acronym is attached to different capital letters to indicate that whatever the capital letter represents is available online.

B&M. Brick and mortar. Refers to physical business locations.

B2B. Business to business.

B2C. Business to customer.

B2G. Business to government.

B2I. Business to Internet.

B2M. Business to machine.

BI. Business intelligence.

BOM. Bill of materials.

BYOD. Bring your own device. Refers to the practice of allowing employees to use their personal electronic devices for work-related activities.

© Copyright sign

C2B. Customer to business.

C2C. Customer to customer.

C2G. Customer (citizen) to government.

C2I. Customer to Internet.

C2M. Customer to machine.

CAR. Corrective action request.

CMYK. Cyan-magenta-yellow-key, a subtractive color management system for printers where the key is normally a black pattern that the other colors are aligned to form a color image. For black text or black portions of images only the key is printed.

CRC. Cyclic redundancy check.

CRM. Customer relationship management.

DGPS. Differential global positioning system.

DPBC. Delivery point bar code.

DSS. Decision support systems.

ERP. Enterprise Resource Planning.

FAQ. Frequently asked question.

FCFS. First-come-first-served. A priority rule for serving customers in the order that they arrive.

FIFO. First-in-first-out. A priority rule for using the oldest inventory first or processing the oldest item in the queue first.

G2B. Government to business.

G2C. Government to customer (citizen).

G2I. Government to Internet.

G2M. Government to machine.

GIGO. Garbage-in-garbage-out. A truism that expresses that your result is only as good as the materials or sources of information you use.

GIS. Geographical information system. Sometimes it is defined as geo-spatial or geographical information science.

GPIB. General purpose interface bus. See **HP-IB**.

GPS. Global positioning system.

 # Hashtag. A metadata symbol used to designate a topic for group discussion that can be more easily searched for.

HP-IB. Hewlett-Packard interface bus, same as GPIB or IEEE-488.

I2B. Internet to business.

I2G. Internet to government.

I2C. Internet to customer.

I2M. Internet to machine.

IaaS. Infrastructure as a service.

IMHO. In my humble opinion. A shorthand notation to tell the reader that the source of the comment is you.

IoT. Internet of things.

IRC. Internet relay chat.

ISBN. International standard book code.

LIFO. Last-in-first-out. A priority rule for serving the last arrival or using the newest inventory first. This rule is not a good idea, but is often used by those who do not manage their inventory wisely or serve their customers fairly.

M2B. Machine to business.

M2C. Machine to customer.

M2G. Machine to government.

M2I. Machine to Internet.

M2M. Machine to machine.

MEGO. My eyes glaze over. Shorthand for the feeling after viewing presentation slides with too much information in small print.

MIS. Management Information Systems.

MRP. Materials requirements planning.

MRP-II. Manufacturing resource planning.

N/A. Not applicable. Useful when the information in a cell in a relational or other structured database is meaningless or not necessary.

NoSQL. Non-relational database designed for large data systems.

OCR. Optical character recognition.

PaaS. Programs available as a service.

PBX. Private branch exchange.

PDM. Product data management.

POS. Point of sale.

QR. Quick response when used as a modifier for code.

® Registered sign

PSTN. Public switched telephone network.

RDBMS. Relational database management system.

RFID. Radio frequency identification.

RGB. Red-green-blue, an additive color management system used for displays and projected images. White is produced by projecting all colors and black is produced by projecting no color.

SaaS. Software available as a service.

SKU. Stock keeping unit.

SMB. Small-to-medium business.

SOP. Sales and operations planning

SPC. Statistical process control.

SQL. Structured query language, used to access relational databases.

™ Trademark sign

TLA. Three-letter acronym.

TQC. Total quality control.

TQM. Total quality management.

UCC. Uniform code council.

UPC. Universal product code.

USB. Universal serial bus.

VBA. Visual Basic for Applications.

VMI. Vendor managed inventory, sometimes called bin stock.

VoIP. Voice over Internet protocol.

VRM. Vendor relationship management.

WAAS. Wide area augmentation system. A method for improving GPS accuracy.

WIP. Work-in-process.

APPENDIX C

Excel Tips and Useful Functions

A significant amount of the content in this appendix is taken from Appendix D in my earlier book on waiting line applications.[1] The content has been updated and augmented with some new content to better serve the discussion of integrating information considerations more thoroughly with other business processes. Readers interested in a more in-depth coverage of process simulation methods using Excel should find the waiting line book a useful companion reference.

Data Analysis Pack

This option in Excel needs to be activated for simulations since many of the functions mentioned require it. It is loaded when the software is installed, but for reasons unknown it is left to a user to activate it. Similarly, Excel's Solver option must also be activated by the user. To activate it, follow the appropriate instructions below.

Excel Version 2003: Select the "Tools" menu, scroll down to the "Add-Ins" choice, select and you will see a list of add-ins. Click the box for Analysis ToolPak. If not already activated, clicking the boxes for the other choices that do not have VBA (Visual Basic for Applications) at the end would be a good idea for future use in business problems. (VBA is for advanced Excel users who wish to program their own special functions). Click OK and return to Excel. The data analysis add-in can then be found as a choice on the Tools menu.

Excel Version 2007: Click on the big button in the upper left corner, select "Excel Options" at the lower right of the menu, then select "Add-Ins" in the left column of choices. Then check to see if the Analysis ToolPak and the Solver Add-in applications are active. If not, click "Go" on the "Manage Excel Add-ins" menu at the bottom and then check the Analysis ToolPak and Solver Add-ins menu that appears and click OK. The Data Analysis and Solver add-ins can then be found on the far right of the Data tab menu.

Excel Version 2010: The instructions are similar to those for Excel 2007, but you select the "File" menu instead of the big button.

Useful Excel Functions

Excel has a fairly good help menu for learning new functions. A good reference to have for quickly learning how to use any given Excel function is the book by Held.[2] Some functions you may find particularly useful are:

IF (condition, true answer, false answer) function. Returns one result if the condition is true (e.g., $X \geq 60$), another if it is false (e.g., $X < 60$). By concatenating IF functions (that is, using another IF function for a true answer and/or a false answer), different sets of outcomes can be determined depending on the input conditions.

COUNTIF (range, criteria) function. Useful for counting the number of values within a defined range in a much larger set of data. An example would be the number of Utah and Nevada residents in a customer address database.

SUMPRODUCT (array1, array2, array3, …array n) function. Useful when the total of a number of products of individual items is desired. An example would be four columns of data: column A listing the name for an item, column B listing the quantity on hand for that item, column C listing the unit cost of that item, and column D listing the inventory tax rate for that item. Therefore, the potential inventory cost for an item is the quantity on hand times the unit cost times the tax rate. To get the total inventory cost without having to calculate individual item costs in a fifth column and then sum that column, one uses the SUMPRODUCT function using the data in columns B, C, and D as three input arrays to get the total in one cell operation. This function is particularly useful when setting up conditions for Excel's Solver to find an optimal solution.

VLOOKUP and **HLOOKUP** functions. These are used to select one piece of data in a table based on a correlating piece of data in that table when there is not an equation that can be used to relate the two values directly. An example would be selecting the arrival rate associated with a given probability of occurrence.

Sparkline Tools. These compact within-a-cell charting functions are available via the "Insert" menu for Excel 2010. See Figure 2.1 in the text for an example of their use.

Conditional Formatting functions. These functions are useful for highlighting various data values according to rules you define. Most Excel users are familiar with highlighting negative values by displaying them in red; these functions expand the range of possibilities by offering data bars, colors, or symbols to highlight values of interest. They are available via the "Styles" submenu on the "Home" menu for Excel 2007 or Excel 2010.

Descriptive Statistics, Histogram, Regression, Rank and **Percentile** functions. These are found in the Data Analysis pack. The other functions provided in the pack are also useful from time to time, but these functions are more commonly needed.

- Descriptive Statistics allows you to just select a range of data values and obtain results such as the average, min, max, standard deviation, median, kurtosis, and so forth, using just one keystroke.
- Histogram sorts the selected data into "bins" (bin sizes can be specified by you) and can also create a histogram chart of the results automatically.
- Regression allows calculating the intercept and slope constants from a set of x and y data for use in a straight-line approximation of this data.
- Rank and Percentile sorts a set of integer data from highest occurrence to lowest and calculates the percentage for each occurrence value as a percent of the whole. This function can be useful for determining probabilities for discrete distributions in simulations.

Inverse Probability Distributions. These expressions are used for simulating operating values using random number (RN) inputs. The Excel function for RN is RAND(). Some of these distributions can also be used in simulating failure probabilities for maintenance service applications or for distributing customer arrivals.

- Exponential Distribution: $t = -(1/(\lambda \text{ or } \mu) \times \ln(\text{RN})$
- Uniform Distribution (min value = a, max value = b): $t = a + \text{RN}$ (b–a); for an equivalent Excel function, use RANDBETWEEN(a,b)
- Normal Distribution[3]: $t = t_{avg} + \sigma[\Sigma_{i=1}^{12} \text{RN}_i - 6]$; for an equivalent Excel function, use NORM.INV(RN,mean,sigma)
- Beta Distribution: Use Excel's BETA.INV(RN,α,β,A,B) function.
- Gamma Distribution (often used instead of Erlang's distribution): Use Excel's GAMMA.INV(RN,α,β) function.
- Log Normal Distribution: Use Excel's LOGNORM.INV(RN, mean, standard_dev) function.

Data Tables. This useful, but obscure capability of Excel is useful for summarizing simulation results. For example, when you run a queueing simulation for 100 customers who might represent a day's work and summarize the results—average line length, average waiting time, max and min values, and so forth, it is laborious to press the F9 key to execute another 100-customer run, repeat the summarization, and so on, to accumulate maybe a month's worth of work. Data tables allow you to collect a number of such summaries with a single press of the F9 key, a major savings in time for simulation analysis. Note: For those of you unfamiliar with this use of the F9 key, pressing it causes Excel to recalculate all of the calculations on the worksheet. This includes selecting new random number values where the RAND() function is used on the worksheet.

Most Excel handbooks are quite vague about how to do this and even finding the software menu for data tables is difficult. In Excel 2010, the menu is part of the "What If Analysis" submenu under the "Data" tab on the toolbar. The book by Weida et al.[4] has a fair introduction to the use of data tables for queuing simulations if you are using an older version of Excel. Chapter 15 of Winston[5] and pages 656–661 of Harvey[6] provide a number of examples on how to set them up for one-way and two-way applications. When you want to apply them to summarizing simulation data, many of the handbooks rarely discuss how to use a variable that is not actually used in the calculations (like the simulation run number) to trigger the number of repetitions desired. Weida et al.[7] does provide some advice as to how to do that, but it can be tricky to make it work right. The other difficulty is that help searches for data tables often assume that you are inquiring about pivot tables and the search takes you there. They are not the same!

It may take some effort to get a data table to work correctly for you, but the effort is well worth it.

Pivot Tables. The advantage of Pivot Tables in Excel is that a variety of ways for depicting tabular information is possible without the need for entering formulas in separate tables of data for calculating averages, medians, and so forth, so that those calculated values can be charted or plotted. Pivot Tables extract the desired data from the tabular information and process that data as desired for either a summary table or a desired graphic output, or both. The processing options are extensive and include filtering, comparing, sorting, logical, math functions, and value testing. If you need to analyze a significant amount of data on a regular basis, becoming proficient in the use of Pivot Tables will be worth your time. I would recommend becoming familiar with the basic Pivot Table functions before downloading the Power-Pivot application from Microsoft®. To be honest, learning how to use Pivot Tables is not a trivial exercise and not to be undertaken for the first time when one is working within a limited time constraint. Some useful references for self-study are the two books by Jelen.[8]

A major disadvantage is that there is no Undo or CTRL-Z function for Pivot Table operations, so mistakes are harder to correct. Pivot Tables also cannot be edited the way other Excel tables can be edited. That is, you cannot insert an extra column or row in a Pivot Table using the "Insert" function. There may be a simple trick for canceling a Pivot Table and starting anew, but I have not found it yet.

Hence, it is a good idea to save a separate file copy of your data, like that shown in Figure C.1, when you are learning how to use Pivot Tables.

To show some of the outputs possible we will consider some typical data collected by a retail business as shown in Figure C.1. This business has two store locations in a city with a population of about 150,000 people. The locations are super-sized convenience stores located near commuter transportation centers. The stores sell popular gift items, some kitchen utensils, household repair items, and gourmet food items in addition to the usual convenience store products of snack food, dairy products, beverages, ready-cooked items, and commonly used over-the-counter medicines. The managers are considering changing the number of hours a location is open,

Time Period	Downtown store customer volume							Westgate store customer volume						
	Sun	Mon	Tue	Wed	Thu	Fri	Sat	Sun	Mon	Tue	Wed	Thu	Fri	Sat
8AM-9 AM	38	47	47	36	39	40	38	42	50	44	52	52	40	52
9AM-10AM	46	41	52	41	36	54	52	64	50	43	41	43	52	48
10 AM-11AM	42	41	57	52	60	50	53	62	67	45	53	60	51	58
11AM-12PM	73	75	59	57	73	62	77	95	82	98	85	79	84	83
12PM-1PM	97	76	95	74	102	97	96	110	108	90	92	112	93	108
1PM-2PM	79	93	76	78	104	81	104	91	93	67	82	76	85	106
2PM-3PM	73	72	62	74	72	84	80	76	67	90	92	84	91	96
3PM-4PM	81	58	73	62	71	73	82	97	102	79	91	100	80	90
4PM-5PM	80	82	86	82	93	85	82	108	109	92	101	91	94	93
5PM 6PM	88	104	106	96	104	83	75	96	124	136	116	135	108	102

Figure C.1. Customer volume and sales volume (next page) for two store locations for a given week.

	Downtown store sales volume							Westgate store sales volume						
Time Period	Sun	Mon	Tue	Wed	Thu	Fri	Sat	Sun	Mon	Tue	Wed	Thu	Fri	Sat
8AM-9 AM	$255	$760	$640	$525	$630	$270	$415	$815	$735	$720	$480	$1,085	$365	$970
9AM-10AM	$1,470	$610	$625	$745	$380	$1,450	$750	$1,025	$1,000	$765	$705	$700	$840	$730
10 AM-11AM	$1,090	$640	$1,185	$1,485	$1,500	$980	$1,495	$1,575	$1,420	$1,715	$1,385	$1,235	$1,090	$1,855
11AM-12PM	$1,785	$1,300	$1,370	$1,310	$1,515	$1,205	$1,745	$2,705	$1,410	$1,405	$1,715	$1,420	$2,110	$1,775
12PM-1PM	$2,460	$1,420	$1,765	$1,570	$2,100	$2,135		$2,380	$2,140	$1,715	$1,375	$2,090	$1,605	$1,860
1PM-2PM	$1,740	$2,000	$1,565	$1,610	$1,635	$1,295	$1,670	$2,350	$1,860	$1,545	$2,400	$1,345	$1,540	$2,695
2PM-3PM	$2,030	$1,165	$1,260	$1,405	$1,760	$1,415	$1,555	$2,000	$1,500	$1,415	$1,890	$1,875	$1,925	$2,525
3PM-4PM	$3,040	$1,420	$1,025	$1,385	$1,270	$1,485	$2,530	$2,385	$2,190	$1,745	$1,765	$2,480	$1,910	$2,355
4PM-5PM	$2,380	$2,190	$1,775	$2,060	$2,015	$1,390	$2,095	$2,885	$2,865	$2,235	$2,410	$2,360	$2,405	$2,895
5PM 6PM	$2,240	$2,200	$2,500	$1,935	$2,415	$1,905	$1,995	$2,635	$2,520	$2,815	$1,980	$3,365	$2,510	$2,155

maybe expanding a location if the demand justifies it, and so forth. To this end, they have collected some POS data for several weeks from the two locations. To keep this example simple, we will look at just two sets of tabular data for each location: the number of customers and the total amount of sales per hour of operation in each store. Some of the possible analysis results are shown in Figure C.2.

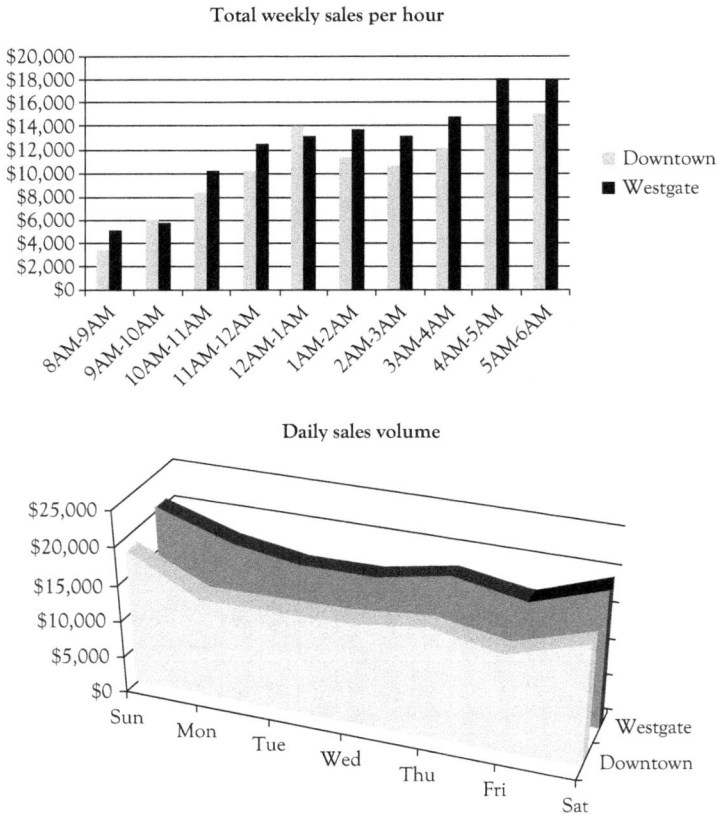

Total weekly sales per hour

Daily sales volume

Figure C.2. Some analysis summaries using the data shown in Figure C.1. When using Pivot Tables to produce these plots, the field buttons must be hidden and some tweaking of the labels is necessary.

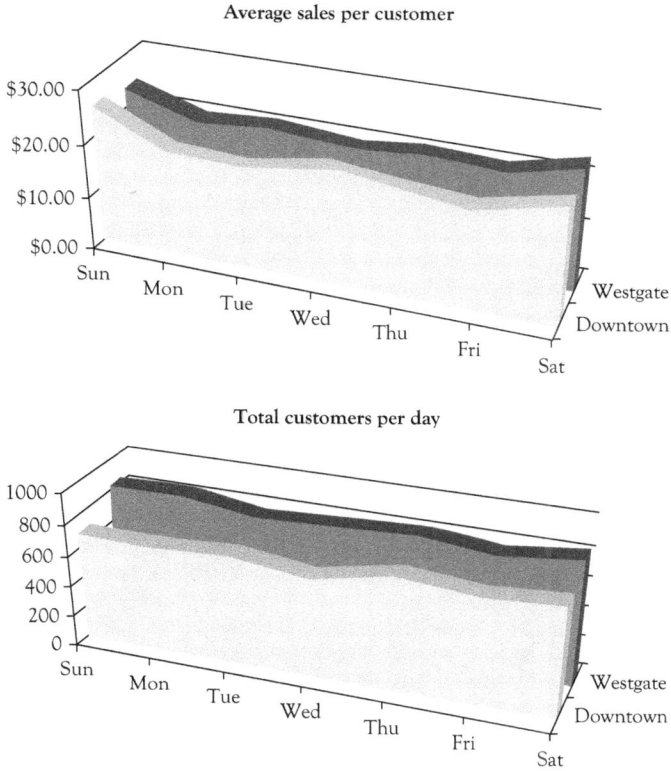

Average sales per customer

Total customers per day

(d)

Figure C.2. Continued.

Some conclusions to be drawn here is that both stores have similar customer and sales patterns with the Westgate store doing slightly better overall because of its higher customer volume. It is interesting to note that weekend customers appear to spend more and sales tend to be higher toward the end of the day. The data suggest that increasing opening hours at the end of the day on weekends might be the best choice for expansion. It is speculation, but maybe weekend commuters have more leisure time to shop and are out later.

Notes

Preface

1. K. Shaw (2011).

Acknowledgments

1. Fitzsimmons & Fitzsimmons (2011).

Chapter 1

1. Training staff how to use more advanced spreadsheet, database, e-mail, and graphics functions should be an integral part of an SMB manager's responsibility. Teaching business students revealed to the author that many of them had not extended their spreadsheet knowledge beyond using such software for row and column accounting tabulations and simple graphs. Their knowledge of the data analysis functions available typically was limited. As a result, it was more difficult to teach them about the uses of a spreadsheet program for decision support applications discussed in chapter 5.
2. The history of Bell Labs by Gertner (2012) is worth a read for those interested in reading more about the history of information technology and other technological advances that helped create the businesses and associated technology we take for granted today. Chapter 7 regarding the contributions of Claude Shannon is particularly appropriate.
3. Felt (1916).
4. Hollerith (1899).
5. One of its many claims to fame is that UNIVAC was used by CBS News to predict the outcome of the presidential election in 1952. However, its correct prediction was not used at first by CBS because their staff doubted it. See Colburn (2012).
6. These two papers were republished in 1949 with an introduction by Warren Weaver as a small paperback book by the University of Illinois Press. This book was reprinted again in 1998 because of the continuing interest in this work.
7. The need for faster transfer of information was illustrated at the beginning of World War II when the tedious manual decoding of Japan's declaration of war on the United States delayed its submission to the US government until after

the attack on Pearl Harbor. No one knows if its more timely submission before the attack would have muted the angry public response and given the US military some time to prepare to reduce the damage.

8. The author's experience with such systems began as the evening operator of a Burroughs Datatron programmed with punched paper tape at Purdue University in 1960 and programming his doctoral research work in FORTRAN IV for a CDC-6400 computer fed with punched cards in 1971.

9. Robat (2012) provides a brief history of software language development. For a more detailed history related to the development of business decision support software, readers are referred to chapter 1 of the book by Power (2013).

10. These differences were often overlooked in the beginning and could cause considerable frustration when one component of a system was upgraded to a newer version that operated much faster. The author programmed a data acquisition system in the late 1960s that had been operating consistently until a new computer with a graphics display replaced an older computer as the system's controller. The variance in output data increased significantly and the system began rejecting more products, yet nothing in manufacturing had been changed to the author's knowledge other than the installation of the new computer. Investigation finally revealed that the cause was the new computer commanding a test module to make a measurement and moving on to the next command to read the measurement result before the test module was able to complete the measurement. The problem was fixed by inserting a BASIC wait command for a few milliseconds delay before sending each read measurement command to allow the test module to complete its operation. The older computer had been slow enough processing commands that these specified delays in the program had not been necessary previously.

11. The old science fiction movies of the 1950s and 1960s often displayed banks of these devices to convey the image of advanced technology. The author was working in the 1960s as part of the engineering team for such tape drives and parts of that technology was later adapted for use in cinema film projectors and other devices using tape media.

12. Christensen (1997). Chapter 1 describes the development of magnetic disk drives for computer storage. The advancements were so rapid that many of the disk drive manufacturers did not survive the transition to the next advance in this technology. Just contrast the five-megabyte storage capacity of IBM's first drive unit in the mid-1950s that was the size of a small refrigerator with today's terabyte storage units that are the size of a small book.

13. In the mid-1970s, the author managed a team developing a 4K memory chip for a major semiconductor manufacturer. As we dealt with the technical

challenges, none of us then would have believed that it would be possible to fabricate the gigabyte plus memory chips available in personal computers and flash drives today.

14. While row-and-column tabulations were available on timesharing mainframes, the level of interactivity to allow individual users to do what-if analysis on their terminals was limited.

15. As more and more routine business activities were made possible on a personal-sized computer, the number of computer terminals and typewriters used by a company began to decline.

16. The author was an editor for technical publications in a corporate marketing department in the early 1980s when a survey was conducted to assess what preferences potential business customers had regarding buying a personal computer. This outside survey listed IBM as one of the potential suppliers although IBM had yet to introduce any version of a personal computer. Not surprisingly, as an example of the power of a brand widely used and trusted, the overwhelming preference by those surveyed was for a computer from IBM because many business were already using IBM mainframes and other equipment such as the Selectric© typewriter used to prepare documents.

17. The Apple Macintosh introduced many users in 1984 to the graphical interface and computer mouse we are familiar with today. Steve Job's fascination with type fonts provided users with choices that help lead users to do graphical design on a computer instead of the traditional pen-and-pencil approach.

18. New Media Institute (2013).

19. The development of satellite technology is a story in its own right. Take a moment to consider how much our global economy depends on satellites monitoring our weather, enabling nearly immediate communication (some time lag because of distance exists) to all parts of the world, and providing information that allows us to readily determine our locations on the globe.

20. On a personal note, I benefitted from this recently when I required an emergency room visit while traveling. While I was checked in for examination, the local doctor was able to retrieve online all necessary medical and insurance information from my home medical clinic. Imagine how difficult that would have been to do and how much time it would have taken two decades ago even with express mail services and telephone access.

21. Many older professionals will remember the office debates comparing the merits and faults of printers using either PCL (printer control language) or Postscript commands. Major printer manufacturers often provided adapter modules to allow their PCL printer to print Postscript formatted documents and vice versa. Ultimately, the software applications evolved to accommodate

different protocols so that users can buy any printer for their use without regard as to what internal control language it uses.

22. Sadly, this situation occurs often enough that faithful readers of Scott Adam's Dilbert© cartoon strip about business activities should readily recognize his "Mordac, the Preventer of Information Services" character representing IT support.

Chapter 2

1. Denning and Bell (2012).
2. Shannon (1948).
3. Stevens (1956 and 1959); Wright (1997); and X-Rite (2007).
4. Stevens (1959).
5. A list of power series expansion approximations for common trigonometric, exponential, and logarithmic functions can be found by a simple search on the Internet. For example, see list at http://mathworld.wolfram.com/SeriesExpansion.html
6. Besides, overall less ink is used with the CMYK approach, particularly when printing text and black ink is often slightly less expensive to produce than the other colors.
7. Tufte (2001).
8. Tufte (1990, 1997, and 2006).
9. These systems were often used in combination with overnight express services at the time because the packets of information for e-mail were often stored up for batch delivery during the night to reduce the considerable long-distance telephone costs incurred. Keep in mind that at that time we did not yet have the extensive infrastructure of microwave links, communication satellites, and cell towers many of us take for granted today.
10. This was particularly true when applying for a mortgage to buy a home in the 1960s through 1980s. For those of us moving to the western United States, mortgage approvals then were often done in a central office located in the eastern United States, necessitating a wait of up to four weeks before an approved contract was received after application. Any need by the approving office for additional information increased that time significantly. The increased use of Federal Express (now known as FedEx) shipments by businesses in the 1980s helped reduce the typical time by 2–3 weeks.
11. Amateur radio operators in the early days could send at higher speeds when they knew each other, and forms of shorthand code for common words and expressions were developed. For a recent article about code speeds, see Cornwell (2008). We can observe a modern version of this

approach with the many abbreviated expressions used in texting and online social media.

12. These three descriptors appeared in an earlier paper by Laney (2001) describing a 3D data management approach.

13. The book by Chaffe-Stengel and Stengel (2011) discusses a number of ways in which variable data can be depicted, collected, and processed to provide results for decision processes.

14. I encountered this issue recently when reviewing a publisher's homework tutorial program supplementing a textbook for business students. I kept getting the wrong answer for a number of more complex programs because the precision I was using was not the same as the program authors. When I pointed out that many business students use Excel and do not round off their input data, we corrected most of the problems by either specifying in the problem what precision to use or by widening the tolerance on the range of correct answers by 2% or 3%.

15. Big Data advocates argue that one should keep a record of such answers because, who knows, there might be an important correlation between those answers and a business objective.

Chapter 3

1. Microsoft® Visio® 2010 was used for all of the process model diagrams because the program offers all of the formats with easy-to-use drag-and-drop symbols to create a desired model quickly.

2. Hebb (2013).

3. Of course, this may be an incorrect assumption if seasonal product offerings cause much more disruption to basic operations than we would expect. How to deal with such a situation will be discussed in a following book, but for now we will assume that such variations have little effect.

4. Beverages are normally not made-to-stock because they can be prepared relatively quickly than cooked items and it is important they be served hot or cold. Maintaining the proper stock level for cooked foods made-to-stock is tricky since the time allowed before their flavor and taste is affected is not very long even when heat lamps are used.

5. Rummler and Brache (1990).

6. This is an important consideration often ignored when improving processes. The identification of value-added steps is often determined from the customer's viewpoint, but some steps of no value to the customer are still necessary to satisfy internal business requirements.

Chapter 4

1. These offerings have helped me service my KitchenAid® mixer, repair the electric brakes on a trailer, review some statistics applications, and learn how to make sausage and bake croissants.

2. Hubbard (2010).

3. Silver (2012).

4. This added information sometimes leads to a conflict with the IT group responsible for maintaining a company's database. Asking an IT group to add information in the database for the operations function just to prevent and solve problems or improve processes is often resisted if it requires increases in storage and processing capacity. This resistance is more likely to be strong if the IT group is held accountable for information processing costs. Such a situation is often resolved by the operations function by setting up their own internal database, a less effective solution from both overall business cost and information integrity viewpoints.

5. Several recent surveys report that the proportion of US citizens owning a smartphone exceeded 50% in 2012 and that smartphones purchases accounted for nearly 52% of total worldwide telephone sales during the same time period.

6. Rand McNally & Company (2008).

7. The inventory of supplies that may be needed to support these service activities is momentarily ignored here. They obviously need tracking and manual entry too, but are only indirectly connected to customer demand.

8. Woodland and Silver (1952).

9. One of my responsibilities during the late 1970s was fabricating Schottky diodes for use in railroad RFID tags. Many of these tags are still in use today and can be observed by motorists waiting for a freight train to pass across the road in front of them. This 3-inch-by-7-inch rectangular device is typically the same color as the frame supporting the rail car and is mounted on the lower right corner of the frame.

10. Brain (2013).

11. Foster (1966).

12. The location can be determined by triangulating the tag's broadcast signal using several readers in different known locations or, more commonly these days, using a small GPS chip attached directly to the tag. Such tags are often used by wildlife study groups to track animals or birds of interest.

13. This capability certainly would have been useful in the days when I was managing R&D and manufacturing groups. Keeping our test equipment calibrated and locating a particular instrument that needed to be returned to

the group or agency that had loaned it to us were frequent activities that often took more time than expected.

14. Although I personally do not approve of this application, the reader-equipped warehouse solution can be used to locate and track employees in large facilities by merely embedding an RFID tag in each of their employee ID badges.

15. IBM (2006).

16. Holloway (2006).

17. Zelbst and Sower (2012).

Chapter 5

1. Laney (2001).

2. During my working career in the high-tech industry, I was asked to solve a number of problems that were created by the cessation or unintentional alteration of ghost processes. Talking to the person who had done the work before the problem occurred was a key factor in finding a solution.

3. Some links to companies offering generic information software applications that could be adapted for use by an SMB without too much effort are listed in the References section under "Information Software Applications: Weblinks." I do not endorse or recommend any of these solutions and only provide their URLs as a potential starting point for a search for an information software solution that best fits your business's needs.

4. If you are interested in learning more about the possible origin of "Big Data," an article by Steve Lohr (2013) in an issue of the *NY Times* is one place to begin.

5. An excellent example of applying Big Data solutions to a large image database was the rapid identification of suspects in the 2013 Boston Marathon bombing. Video and still photos were collected from a wide range of sources such as cell phones, security cameras, and newscast footage for the analysis and processed very quickly.

6. This term came into use in the early 1970s. For a more detailed history of the development of decision support systems, see the introduction by Power (2013).

7. Chapter 9 in Evans (2010) discusses the application of a number of such tools available in Excel for decision models.

8. Chaffe-Stengel and Stengel (2011).

9. Power (2013).

10. Kroenke (2011).

11. Baltzan et al. (2009).

12. Beaseley (n.d.).
13. Wailgum (2009).
14. A word to the wise manager: In some larger corporations this passive resistance can go as far as a department maintaining a duplicate database for local use or even continuing to use the old processes to do things while feeding the ERP system just enough data to keep it happy. This fact should not be too shocking because those of us who have worked as individual contributors in large organizations have all known of a group that at some time would shape up temporarily to pass a quality audit or other regularly scheduled inspection and then return to business as usual after the inspector left. When you become a manager or inspector, part of your basic responsibilities is to prevent this from happening or at least catch it when it does.
15. Shaw (2011).
16. Copy of Example 6.5 taken from Shaw (2011), pp. 96–97.
17. Pinedo (2008).
18. Recall the discussion regarding Shannon's communication model shown in Fig. 1.1b
19. Stein and Katzenberg (circa mid-2000s).
20. If you are interested in learning more about the history of the PicturePhone, the following website is a good place to start: http://www.beatriceco.com/bti/porticus/bell/telephones-picturephone.html
21. http://www.usbr.gov/projects/Project.jsp?proj_Name=Colorado%20River%20Basin%20Project&pageType=ProjectPage
22. http://www.ecy.wa.gov/programs/wr/cwp/ops.html

Chapter 6

1. The old-time metal safe with the company's ledger book inside comes to mind here.
2. The stated range for these devices is a conservative value that guarantees suitable reception within that range for all sorts of local conditions. The units on our farm in a rural area reliably access devices in outbuildings up to 200 feet away, and on some days I can even detect some neighbor's wireless network even though the nearest neighbor is at least 1,200 feet from our house. However, a repeater is still needed for a reliable connection between devices on our upstairs and downstairs floors.
3. There are a number of password strength checkers available online such as the one at https://www.microsoft.com/en-gb/security/pc-security/password-checker.aspx

4. This knowledge is useful to know in the event that one accidentally erases the only copy of some critical data and they failed to do a backup recently. Stop immediately before any new data are written to the disk and take your computer to a recovery expert to get the critical data back.
5. The author is speaking from personal experiences purchasing and selling properties in different states and counties during his life. While the retrieval processes are much better most agencies, the incompatibility between their databases and record systems remains the same.
6. Hubbard (2010).

Appendix A

1. In the early days of the World Wide Web when landline telephone systems were used for access, these collections and discussions were often referred to as bulletin boards or user forums.
2. This is often referred to as a swim-lane or Rummler–Brache (1990) diagram based on assigning a column or row for each functional area. This allows easier identification of communication needs between functions and how heavily that function is loaded. A similar approach is the service blueprint used to map customer interactions.
3. In more sophisticated treatments of front office activities, the steps are separated into two subgroups: those that require the participation of every customer served and those that may require further participation by some customers.
4. Little (1961). The proof of this relation was published first by Little, although others had used it without proof prior to his paper.

Appendix C

1. Shaw (2011).
2. Held (2007).
3. See Fitzsimmons and Fitzsimmons (2011), page 438 for the reasoning behind the derivation of this expression. For a more convenient method than using 12 random numbers for each value required, use Excel's NORM.INV function.
4. Weida et al. (2001).
5. Winston (2004).
6. Harvey (2007).
7. Weida et al. (2001).
8. Jelen (2010, 2011).

References and Bibliography

Foreword: Some useful references from the Internet are listed among the more traditional book and periodical references below; using their titles in search engines as starting points are more likely to lead to the types of articles you are looking for. While most of the references are cited where appropriate in the text, some are not. I found these noncited references to be useful in developing a general overview of major topics and many of them have good examples illustrating the use and processing of information to support business decisions.

Baltzan, P., Phillips, A., & Haag, S. (2009). *Business driven technology* (3rd ed.). New York, NY: McGraw-Hill/Irwin.

Beaseley, J. R. (no date). *Materials requirements planning (MRP)*. Retrieved June 9, 2013 from http://people.brunel.ac.uk/~mastjjb/jeb/or/mrp.html

Bozarth, C. C., & Handfield, R. B. (2008). *Introduction to operations and supply chain management* (2nd ed.). Upper Saddle River, NJ: Prentice Hall.

Brain, M. (2013). *How UPC bar codes work.* Retrieved February 22, 2013, from http://electronics.howstuffworks.com/gadgets/high-tech-gadgets/upc1.htm

Chaffe-Stengel, P., & Stengel, D. N. (2011). *Working with sample data.* New York, NY: Business Expert Press.

Christensen, C. M. (1997). *The innovator's dilemma.* Boston, MA: Harvard Business School Press.

Colburn, R. (2012). *A correct prediction so surprising it would not be believed—UNIVAC and the 1952 Presidential Election.* Retrieved March 23, 2013, from http://www.todaysengineer.org/2012/Oct/history.asp

Coldewey, D. (2012). There's so much data that we're running out of words to describe it. *NBC NEWS*. Retrieved December 12, 2012, from http://www.nbcnews.com/technology/futureoftech/theres-so-much-data-were-running-out-words-describe-it-1C7557410

Computer History Museum—Timeline of Computer History (2013). Retrieved February 14, 2013, from http://www.computerhistory.org/timeline/?category=cmptr

Cornwell, J. M. (2008). Morse code at 140 WPM. *American Radio Relay League*. Retrieved February 26, 2013, from http://www.arrl.org/news/morse-code-at-140-wpm

Denning, P. J., & Bell, T. (2012). The information paradox. *American Scientist 100* (November–December), 470–477.

ERP Software Systems Index for Manufacturing. Top10ERP. Retrieved December 12, 2012, from http://www.top10erp.org/.

Evans, J. R. (2010). *Statistics, data analysis, and decision modeling* (4th ed.). Upper Saddle River, NJ: Prentice Hall

Felt, D. E (1916). *Mechanical arithmetic, or the history of the counting machine*. Chicago, IL: Washington Institute. Retrieved March 23, 2013, from http://archive.org/stream/mechanicalarithm00feltrich#page/n1/mode/2up

Fitzsimmons, J. A., & Fitzsimmons, M. J. (2011). *Service management: Operations, strategy, information technology* (7th ed.). New York, NY: McGraw-Hill.

Foster, F. G. (1966). *Standard numbering in the book trade*. Retrieved June 7, 2013, from http://web.archive.org/web/20110430024722/http://www.informaticsdevelopmentinstitute.net/isbn.html

Fung, K. (2010). *Numbers rule your world*. New York, NY: McGraw-Hill.

Gertner, J. (2012). *The idea factory*. New York, NY: The Penguin Press

Harkins, S. (2009). Use Excel's built-in features to simplify data entry. *TechRepublic.com*. Retrieved May 27, 2013, from: http://www.techrepublic.com/blog/msoffice/use-excels-built-in-features-to-simplify-data-entry/999

Harrison, G. (2010). *10 things you should know about NoSQL databases*. TechRepublic.com. Retrieved May 27, 2013, from http://www.techrepublic.com/blog/10things/10-things-you-should-know-about-nosql-databases/1772

Harvy, G. (2007). *Excel® 2007 All-in-one desk reference for dummies.* Indianapolis, IN: Wiley Publishing Inc.

Hebb, N. (2013). Flowchart symbols defined. *Breezetree.com.* Retrieved May 24, 2013, from http://www.breezetree.com/article-excel-flow chart-shapes.htm

Heizer, J., & Render, B. (2008). *Operations management* (9th ed.). Upper Saddle River, NJ: Prentice Hall.

Held, B. (2007). *Microsoft® Excel® functions & formulas.* Plano, TX: Wordware Publishing, Inc.

Heyde, C. C., & Seneta, E., editors (2001). *Statisticians of the centuries.* New York, NY: Springer-Verlag.

Hillier, F. S., & Lieberman, G. J. (2010). *Introduction to operations research* (9th ed.). New York, NY: McGraw-Hill.

Holloway, S. (2006). *RFID: An introduction.* Retrieved June 6, 2013, from http://msdn.microsoft.com/en-us/library/aa479355.aspx

Hollerith, H. (1899). An electric tabulating system. *The Quarterly, Columbia University School of Mines 10*(16), 238–255. Retrieved March 23, 2013, from http://www.columbia.edu/cu/computinghistory/hh/index.html

Hubbard, D. W. (2010). *How to measure anything* (2nd ed.). Hoboken, NJ: John Wiley & Sons, Inc.

IBM (2006). RFID supermarket TV commercial. Retrieved June 6, 2013, from http://www.youtube.com/watch?v=eob532iEpqk

Information Software Application Vendors: Weblinks as of June 10, 2013, http://www.cybertec.it/en/index.html
http://www54.sap.com/solution.html
http://www.jda.com/solutions/solutions-index/
http://www.infor.com/
http://www.quintiq.com/solutions.aspx
http://www.rfidusa.com/

International Organization for Standardization (May 2009). *ISO DRG directives* (2nd ed.). Retrieved December 11, 2012, from http://www.iso.org/iso/drginstr.pdf.

Jacobs, F. R., & Chase, R. B. (2011). *Operations and supply chain management* (13th ed.). New York, NY: McGraw-Hill.

Jelen, B. (2010). *PowerPivot for the data analyst: Microsoft® Excel®2010.* Indianapolis, IN: Que Publishing.

Jelen, B. (2011). *Charts and graphs: Microsoft® Excel®2010.* Indianapolis, IN: Que Publishing.

Kincaid, J. W. (2003). *Customer relationship management.* Upper Saddle River, NJ: Prentice Hall PTR.

Krajewski, L. J., Ritzman, L. P., & Malhotra, M. K. (2010). *Operations management: Processes and supply chains* (9th ed.). Upper Saddle River, NJ: Prentice Hall.

Kroenke, D. M. (2011). *Using MIS* (3rd ed.). Upper Saddle River, NJ: Prentice Hall.

Laguna, M., & Marklund, J. (2005). *Business process modeling, simulation, and design.* Upper Saddle River, NJ: Prentice-Hall

Laney, D. (2001). 3D data management: Controlling data volume, velocity, and variety. *Application Delivery Strategies*, META Group, File 949, February 6, 2001. Retrieved May 26, 2013 from: http://blogs.gartner.com/doug-laney/files/2012/01/ad949-3D-Data-Management-Controlling-Data-Volume-Velocity-and-Variety.pdf

Little, J. D. C. (1961). A proof of the queuing formula: L = λW. *Operations Research 9*(3), 383–387.

Lohr, S. (2013). Searching for origins of the term "Big Data." *New York Times*, New York edition, B4, February 4, 2013. Retrieved May 26, 2013, from http://bits.blogs.nytimes.com/2013/02/01/the-origins-of-big-data-an-etymological-detective-story/

McMullen, B. S., & Monsere, C. (2010). *Freight performance measures: Approach analysis.* SPR 664 OTREC-RR-10-04 Retrieved February 26, 2013, from http://ntl.bts.gov/lib/33000/33000/33025/Freight_Performance_Measures.pdf

Nelson, B. L. (2010). *Stochastic modeling: analysis & simulation.* Mineola, NY: Dover Publications, Inc.

New Media Institute (2013). *History of the Internet.* Retrieved February 18, 2013, from http://www.newmedia.org/history-of-the-internet.html

Pinedo, M. L. (2008). Scheduling: Theory, algorithms, and systems (3rd ed.). New York, NY: Springer Science+Business Media, LLC. Support websites: http://extras.springer.com and http://www.stern.nyu.edu/~mpinedo

Power, D. J. (2013). *Decision support, analytics, and business intelligence* (2nd ed.). New York, NY: Business Expert Press.

Rand McNally & Company (2008). *2009 Commercial atlas & marketing guide* (140th ed.). Skokie, IL: Rand McNally & Co.

Rasch Measurement Transactions Contents. *A collection of articles on measurement philosophy and methods available for free* at http://www.rasch.org/rmt/contents.htm

Robat, C. (Ed.) (2012). *Introduction to software history*. Retrieved February 14, 2013, from http://www.thocp.net/software/software_reference/introduction_to_software_history.htm#how

Ross, S. M. (2010). *Introduction to probability models* (10*th* ed.). Burlington, MA: Academic Press. *Author's note: This is a useful reference for those readers who are comfortable working with mathematic notation and concepts at a higher level than most of the content in this monograph.*

Rummler, G. A., & Brache, A. P. (1990). *Improving performance.* San Francisco, CA: Jossey-Bass Publishers.

Shannon, C. E. (1948). A mathematical theory of communication. *Bell System Technical Journal 27*(3), July/October, 379–423.

Shannon, C. E., & Weaver, W. (1949). *The mathematical theory of communication.* Urbana and Chicago, IL: University of Illinois Press – www.press.uillinois.edu Reprinted 1998.

Shaw, K. A. (2011). *Operations methods: Waiting line applications.* New York, NY: Business Expert Press.

Shostack, G. L. (1984). Designing services that deliver. *Harvard Business Review*, January-February, 133–139. Retrieved July 27, 2011, from http://www.semanticfoundry.com/docs/servicesThatDeliver.pdf

Silver, N. (2012). *The signal and the noise.* New York, NY: Penguin Press.

Stein, B., & Katzenberg, J. (circa mid-2000s). *HP Halo video.* Retrieved June 10, 2013, from http://h20621.www2.hp.com/video-gallery/us/en/FEEDROOM169105/r/video

Stevens, S. S. (1946). On the theory of scales of measurement. *Science 103* (2684), June 7, 677–680.

Stevens, S. S. (1959). Measurement, psychophysics and utility, Chap. 2. In C. W. Churchman, & P. Ratoosh (Eds.), *Measurement: Definitions and theories.* New York, NY: John Wiley

Stevenson, W. J. (2011). *Operations management* (11th ed.). New York, NY: McGraw-Hill.

Tufte, E. R. (1990). *Envisioning information.* Cheshire, CN: Graphics Press.

Tufte, E. R. (1997). *Visual explanations.* Cheshire, CN: Graphics Press.

Tufte, E. R. (2001). *The visual display of quantitative information* (2nd ed.). Cheshire, CN: Graphics Press.

Tufte, E. R. (2006). *Beautiful evidence.* Cheshire, CN: Graphics Press.

Turing, A. M. (1936). On computable numbers, with an application to the Entscheidungs problem. *Proceedings of the London Mathematical Society 2 42* (1): 230–265. United States Broadband Map. http://www.broadbandmap.gov/

Wailgum, T. (2009). *10 famous ERP disasters, dustups and disappointments.* Retrieved June 9, 2013, from http://www.cio.com/article/print/486284

Walkenbach, J. (2010). *John Walkenbach's favorite Excel® 2010 tips & tricks.* Indianapolis, IN: Wiley Publishing Inc.

Weida, N. C., Richardson, R., & Vazsonyi, A. (2001). *Operations analysis using Microsoft® Excel.* Pacific Grove, CA: Duxbury—Thomson Learning.

Winston, W. L. (2004). *Microsoft® Excel data analysis and business modeling.* Redmond, WA: Microsoft Press.

Woodland, N. J., & Silver, B. (1952). *Classifying apparatus and method.* US Patent 2,612,994, issued October 7, 1952.

Wright, B. D., (1997). S.S. Stevens revisited. *Rasch Measurement Transactions 11*(1), 552–553. Retrieved February 24, 2013, from http://www.rasch.org/rmt/rmt111n.htm

X-Rite, Incorporated, (2007). *A guide to understanding color communication.* Retrieved May 16, 2013, from http://www.xrite.com/documents/literature/en/L10-001_Understand_Color_en.pdf

Zelbst, P., & Sower, V. (2012). *RFID for the operations and supply chain professional.* New York, NY: Business Expert Press.

Zikopoulos, P. C., Eaton, C., deRoos, D., Deutsch, T., & Lapis, G. (2012). *Understanding Big Data.* New York, NY: McGraw-Hill.

Ziff-Davis Business to Business Network, http://b2b.ziffdavis.com/pages/index

Index

OTHER TITLES IN OUR FINANCE AND FINANCIAL MANAGEMENT COLLECTION

Quantitative Approaches to Decision Making Donald Stengel,
California State University, Fresno, Editor

- *Working With Sample Data Exploration and Inference* by Priscilla Chaffe-Stengel and Donald N. Stengel
- *Business Applications of Multiple Regression* by Ronny Richardson
- *Operations Methods Waiting Line Applications* by Ken Shaw
- *Regression Analysis Understanding and Building Business and Economic Models Using Excel* by J. Wilson, Keating Holton, P. Barry, and Mary Beal-Hodges

ALSO IN FORTHCOMING IN THIS COLLECTION

- *Forecasting Across the Organization* by Ozgun Caliskan Demirag, Diane Parente, and Carol L. Putman 12/31/2013
- *Business Applications of Operations Research* by Bodhibrata Nag 2/15/2014
- *Effective Applications of Statistical Process Contro* by Ken Shaw l4/15/2014
- *Leveraging Business Analysis for Project Success* by Vicki James 5/15/2014
- *Construction Projects and the Power of Design-Build: Ensuring Safety and Control in Project Delivery using the SAFEDB Methodology* by Sherif Hashem 6/15/2014
- *Project Risk Concepts, Process, and Tools* by Tom R. Wielicki, and Donald N. Stengel 7/15/2014
- *Effective Applications of Supply Chain Logistics* by Ken Shaw 7/15/2014
- *Working with Time Series Data Analysis and Forecasting* by Donald Stengel, and Priscilla Chaffe-Stengel 8/15/2014
- *Mathematical Modeling in Business and Economics: A Data-Driven Approach* by Rhonda Aull-Hyde 9/15/2014
- *Applied Decision Analysis for Environmental Remediation, Restoration, and Sustainability Projects* by Timothy Havranek and Leigh Hostetter 8/15/2014

Announcing the Business Expert Press Digital Library

Concise E-books Business Students
Need for Classroom and Research

This book can also be purchased in an e-book collection by your library as
- a one-time purchase,
- that is owned forever,
- allows for simultaneous readers,
- has no restrictions on printing, and
- can be downloaded as PDFs from within the library community.

Our digital library collections are a great solution to beat the rising cost of textbooks. e-books can be loaded into their course management systems or onto student's e-book readers.

The **Business Expert Press** digital libraries are very affordable, with no obligation to buy in future years. For more information, please visit **www.businessexpertpress.com/librarians**. To set up a trial in the United States, please contact **Adam Chesler** at *adam.chesler@businessexpertpress.com* for all other regions, contact **Nicole Lee** at *nicole.lee@igroupnet.com*.

www.ingramcontent.com/pod-product-compliance
Lightning Source LLC
Chambersburg PA
CBHW060534210326
41519CB00014B/3221